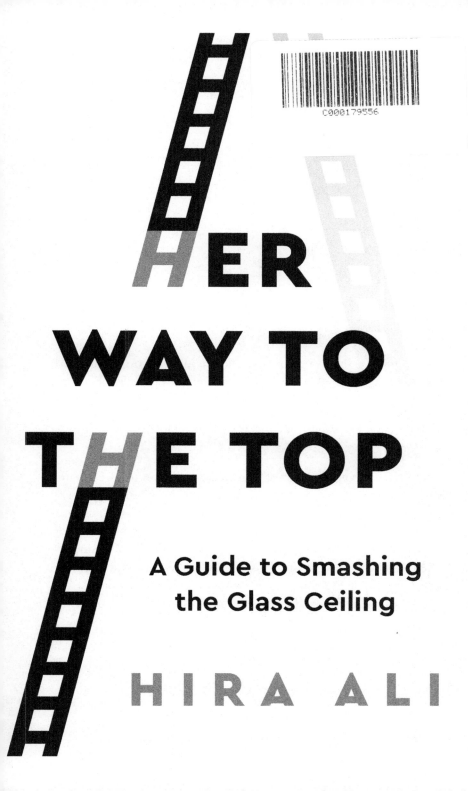

HER
WAY TO
THE TOP

A Guide to Smashing
the Glass Ceiling

HIRA ALI

HER WAY TO THE TOP

First published in 2019 by

Panoma Press Ltd
48 St Vincent Drive, St Albans, Herts, AL1 5SJ, UK
info@panomapress.com
www.panomapress.com

Book layout by Neil Coe.

Printed on acid-free paper from managed forests.

ISBN 978-1-784521-51-6

The right of Hira Ali to be identified as the author of this work has been asserted in accordance with sections 77 and 78 of the Copyright, Designs and Patents Act 1988.

A CIP catalogue record for this book is available from the British Library.

This book is available online and in bookstores.

DEDICATION

This book is dedicated to my parents to whom I owe much of my personal and professional success. They both have made an outstanding contribution to my life and are the ones responsible for getting this woman to the top.

TESTIMONIALS

'By making use of thorough research, concrete suggestions and interesting personal anecdotes, Hira provides an effective and much needed blueprint for women across the globe to prosper and reach the top.'

Marshall Goldsmith, #1 New York Times bestselling author of *Triggers*, *MOJO* **and** *What Got You Here Won't Get You There*

'Hira Ali, an enthusiastic champion of gender equality in the workplace, brings a personal and much welcome international perspective to the challenges facing women seeking to make it to the top in their professional lives. Drawing on her own journey and that of scores of other women around the world, she plots a course for women everywhere to break through the glass ceiling and thrive. Her passion for helping other women overcome internal and external barriers to the top rings loudly throughout.'

Valerie Young, author of *The Secret Thoughts of Successful Women*

'Good research, great illustrative anecdotes, and tangible suggestions for overcoming your stickiest career challenges, make this book a joy to read! Ali manages to convey a depth of understanding of the issues in a way that every woman can learn from and no woman should miss. Her refreshing approach is applicable to women from Anchorage to Zurich and everywhere in between.'

Lois P. Frankel, Ph.D., author of *Nice Girls Don't Get the Corner Office*

'I loved reading *Her Way to the Top* because what Hira describes as her own struggle and the struggle of the women she interviewed speaks to me, like it will to all other women. This is what Hira cleverly explores, the many facets that block us from reaching the top so that we can build a new awareness and arm ourselves to move up in the future. In today's world it is important to know that we are not alone and that we are not the only ones facing this. The thorough choice of topics is incredibly pertinent and universal for women in the business world. I also loved how the practical coping strategies can be implemented right away into my life. The book is well worth reading and exploring for all women who want to rise to the places they deserve.'

**Chiara Condi, activist and entrepreneur,
founder of Led By HER**

'The book is well written and full of interesting, helpful, personal experiences and facts.'

**Carole Stone, CBE, campaigner, broadcaster and
author of *Networking: The Art of Making Friends***

Women careerists need every opportunity to learn new and innovative ways to tackle the roadblocks to the top. Hira Ali's, *Her Way To The Top* comes from a different viewpoint and provides just that. A real thought leader, she tackles head-on the ongoing challenges women regularly face on their way to the top and provides detailed answers to each hurdle. *Her Way To The Top* is a book that all serious career women should read at least once and then pass it on to someone she knows who is travelling the same path.

**Dr. Yvonne Thompson CBE, bestselling author of
*7 Traits Of Highly Successful Women On Boards - View From
The Top and How To Get There.***

ACKNOWLEDGEMENTS

My husband for believing in me and staying by my side throughout everything. His unconditional support in my career has been phenomenal.

My son for being my major source of motivation. His avid interest in this book journey and his endearing daily query, "Mama, is it finished yet?" is what kept me going.

My family members, to whom I owe a ton of gratitude for their unwavering support as well as their appreciation, critique and concern.

My friends who play an active role in helping preserve my sanity.

My professional contacts, coaches and mentors for all their support, advice and valuable suggestions/mentoring.

Last, but definitely not least, my book coach, Liz Buckley, who offered me exceptional support, and my publishing team for turning this dream into a reality.

PREFACE

The intention to write this book began last year, a year into my move to London.

After training women for 13 years, I began to notice a trend among the internal obstacles women face in their career path. When I was in Pakistan, I believed the challenges women faced were background specific and only pertinent to women from developing nations in South East Asia.

And then I moved to Dubai…

I continued seeing the same common trends which led me to wrongly attribute that to the similarities between the Middle Eastern and Asian cultures. Yet Dubai is a multicultural city comprising 85% expats, which helped me realise that even European and American women share similar professional issues. But then again, where you live does have an impact on behaviour patterns, doesn't it?

And then I moved to London… But guess what? Same challenges!

By this time, I had developed a strong online presence and had started to reach out to an international audience via online training and coaching programmes. As a truly progressive city, I believed London would have more empowered women breaking glass ceilings versus struggling with a pay gap, equal representation and infrequent promotions issues, typically affecting women in third world countries. Yet I discovered that even female London professionals faced similar challenges as their global counterparts. A lot has to do with culture and male chauvinism, but in fairness, there are some challenges like gender-specific derailers that also hold women back.

In my podcast interview with Sally Hubbard for *Women Killing It*, I highlighted this observation. I pointed out that professional women across the globe, irrespective of their background, share similar strengths and challenges; thus the traits in women that either make them successful or hold them back are more gender specific than background specific. However, I still had my doubts and was curious to test my theory in greater depth. And that's when I decided to conduct a survey. More than 300 women from various regions responded to one simple question: What are the top challenges holding you back in your career?

The results were astoundingly similar irrespective of background and nationality. Impostor Syndrome and the confidence gap was universally acknowledged as a challenge for all women except Asian women. Impostor Syndrome can be defined as a collection of feelings of inadequacy and self-doubt that persist despite evident success.

Over half of the women reported that Impostor Syndrome regularly plagued them at work. American women reported the highest case of Impostor Syndrome followed by British women.

Perhaps the reason why it didn't score as high in some places was not because it didn't exist, but because people didn't understand the term. When I explained what exactly Impostor Syndrome is, more women could relate to the issue. Also, in Asian countries, women are so busy fighting harsh misogynic work environments that they have little room left for self-doubt. Asian and black women working outside their home country as expats or immigrants, however, again reported a high level of Impostor Syndrome.

Asian and Middle Eastern women noted that FOMO – the Fear Of Missing Out – was one of their biggest challenges. In fact, FOMO was the number one challenge reported by women across all regions, especially working mothers who feared missing out on the responsibilities of their different roles, be it wife, mum, working/businesswoman, daughter or friend. Only a few Asian women reported lack of a support system as a major issue, perhaps because many Asian women live within a joint family system where children are taken care of by grandparents, uncles and aunties. Plus, help is readily available. However, Asian women faced greater external challenges such as misogynist work environments, sexual harassment, and families discouraging career pursuits. Stress and exhaustion seemed to be another factor negatively impacting women universally; women are still expected to do the lion's share of household work and parenting duties, whether women belong to developed/progressive countries or not.

British mums seem be most impacted by planning, organising and timing issues. And considering how expensive childcare is, it's no surprise that managing time efficiently is such a challenge; women in the UK are doing everything all by themselves, with little or no support.

Like FOMO, perfectionism and an inability to self-promote were other universal challenges.

Many of these challenges women face are gender specific, and perhaps that's why the global survey results were so similar. Women process things differently from men and behave differently as well; ie men are more self-oriented while women are more community focused. Women's decision-making processes, along with the dynamics and subtleties of their personalities and style, are qualities unique to them. But unfortunately, these differences can also hold some women back. Although there are certainly gender-neutral challenges, there is a unique set of gender-specific derailers predominantly faced by *women alone*. Often these female-specific challenges are internal obstacles that are rarely discussed.

In this book, I will be examining these core internal and external challenges revealed by the survey. I will also be sharing anecdotes from real women who faced these challenges, along with strategies to overcome them.

Most of the female survey respondents have related internal challenges. Social conditioning has given birth to FOMO and Impostor Syndrome. That fear and self-doubt makes us expend inordinate amounts of effort towards achieving perfection while ensuring no task falls through the cracks. This, in turn, leads to time poverty, stress and exhaustion.

When I was compiling the research for this book, I read the work of several renowned authors who have already explored these internal challenges. In her international best-seller, *Nice Girls Don't Get the Corner Office*, Lois Frankel points out that although both men and women make plenty of mistakes that hold them back, there are unique sets of mistakes predominantly made by women. As Frankel notes: "Whether I am working in Jakarta, Oslo, Prague, Frankfurt, Trinidad or Houston, I am amazed to watch women across cultures make the same mistakes at work. They may be more exaggerated in Hong Kong than in LA, but they are variations on the same theme."

Facebook Chief Operating Officer and billionaire Sheryl Sandberg advised working women to 'lean in' within her book. She writes: "Internal obstacles are rarely discussed and often underplayed. Throughout my life, I was told over and over again about inequalities in the workplace and how hard it would be to have a family and career. I rarely heard anything, however, about the ways I hold myself back. These internal obstacles deserve a lot more attention, in part because they are under our own control. We can dismantle the hurdles in ourselves today. We can start this very moment."

In *The Confidence Code: The Science and Art of Self-Assurance – What Women Should Know*, authors Katty Kay and Claire Shipman wrote: "Underqualified and underprepared men don't think twice about leaning in. Overqualified and overprepared, too many women still hold back. And the confidence gap is an additional lens through which to consider why it is women don't lean in."

But wait… don't get ahead of yourself. Don't automatically assume that it's only you or that it's all in your head. It's not. Many times, these internal obstacles are a result of our social conditioning and external challenges such as gendered work environments or even gendered upbringing that are difficult to ignore. We often place a significant amount of responsibility on ourselves. Many women have been brought up to refrain from questioning the status quo. Making sacrifices as a daughter, wife and mother is ingrained in us early on, and 'Change begins with you' teachings have sometimes tainted our perspectives – we are expected to let go of others and focus on what we can do ourselves. I am guilty of this too.

When I conducted my survey, I listed several challenges holding women back, but almost all challenges were internal ones. I did not add external challenges to the list. And trust me, most women didn't point that out! Only a few women noted that, in addition to internal challenges, misogynistic work environments also hold them back. My response to that was, well, yes, they do, but the survey is about how we hold ourselves back with our own internal challenges. However, there is no denying that most of the internal challenges we face are actually an indirect or direct consequence of gendered work environments and gendered upbringing.

Jessica Valenti, a feminist author and *Guardian* columnist, calls the confidence gap a sham. She says that women's lack of confidence could be just a keen understanding of just how little society values them. "What's the code for that?" she asks when talking about creating a culture that values self-assured women.

In her blog *Why we need to ditch fix the women solutions,* Michelle King says: "Women did what was asked. We got the mentors. We got the sponsors. We attended the development programmes. At some point, we need to give up and accept that these solutions will not solve the issue of gender inequality in the workplace. If we want employees to create, innovate and produce we need work environments that support this. Solving the issue of gender inequality in the workplace starts with understanding what needs to be fixed – and it is not women."

Laura Guillen, digital designer at Harvard Business Review, believes popular messaging that women must change to appear more self-confident and realise success is false. She notes that such thinking also reflects how the burden of managing a gender-diverse workplace is placed on female employees themselves. While their male colleagues focus on personal objectives and are held to lower standards, women are also expected to care for others and thus are shouldering an unfair load. "This prosocial (double) standard does not appear in any job description but it is, indeed, the key performance indicator against which access, power and influence will be granted to successful women."

In my survey, many women responded with their own opinions.

Rose recognises that: "If a person or workplace structure is preventing our advancement, no amount of self-coaching can overcome that very real barrier; to ignore it would be unhealthy and counterproductive. Institutionalised gendering/misogyny must be tackled simultaneously with our own personal/professional development."

Sue Rinde says: "I believe this is how women are socialised. It's not considered as acceptable for women to seek recognition or money, or even to say no to a request at work. I would say most of the women I know work harder for less than most men. And they do not complain."

Cathy reveals that she experiences Impostor Syndrome, but only because the men in charge constantly minimise her contributions and refuse to give her credit for doing good work. Girls and women are generally socialised to be 'less than'.

Seana shares that she knew her male colleagues with less experience were making £30,000 more a year. She challenged the pay inequality and successfully managed to negotiate a salary increase and promotion to a senior executive position. However, she was terrified she might get canned for challenging management.

So, in light of the above observations, shouldn't we work backwards and instead, fix the system and environments that breed these internal challenges – aka gender-specific derailers – in the first place?

In an ideal world, yes! However, according to a report published by Ernst & Young, gender parity (meaning an equal number of men and women) at work will take another 213 years. So, what do we do until then?

In the above comments, there are valid points which cannot be denied, but I think it's also fair to say there is a spectrum of experiences. Many women are pursuing the careers they want to regardless of gender stereotyping, but there are others who struggle to be assertive because they have been conditioned how to behave. This conditioning has given rise to gender-specific career derailers. If these women learn strategies to conquer these challenges, aren't these small positive shifts worth the time? Should everyone just give up on making small improvements in favour of living in a kind of post-patriarchal utopia? I think not.

Many women from my survey were of the view that it's up to us and we should take matters in our own hands. Jana stated: "I believe that misogyny must be combated whenever it rears its ugly head. I feel this is best done by getting your own house in order first so that you recognise what is going on."

Deb said that she was always taught to lead by example. When she began her career, it was a predominantly male profession and she dealt with a lot of discrimination until she quietly demonstrated that she could 'hold her own'. Her job is physically demanding. Most of the places she worked were remote so there was a lack of amenities. She proved that she could 'pioneer' just as well as 'the guys', and most of them remember that.

I have recruited, managed, coached and trained hundreds of women at work. In doing so, I have noticed a 'female confidence gap'. And this shortage of female confidence is not a myth, it is quantified and documented. Young women coming into work are (generally) less assertive, less pushy, and less arrogant than their more seasoned female colleagues. I don't necessarily think this is a bad thing, of course, and my survey reveals the same. But how we rise above these gendered work environments can be up to us and how we choose to respond.

I don't know about you, but I don't want to be a bitter feminist who blames everyone for inequality rather than empowering her own self first. And as much I'd love to change the world, my circle of influence is the strongest around myself. Yes, I want to build more inclusive work environments and play my part by making a difference. But at the end of the day, I was, I am and I always will be my own best rescuer. And I do want to be that strong feminist, or 'equalist', who will rescue her own self first. I strongly believe that by conquering our internal challenges we will be better equipped to deal with the external ones. Because whether the challenge is internal or external, change does begin with you. This book covers a lot about what *you* can do to empower yourself and kick start your progress! So, let's get on with that, shall we?

Survey Methodology

I launched an online social media poll to survey women from Asia, including the Middle East, Europe, Canada, Australia, Africa, the United Kingdom and the United States of America.

Some women chose to share their response along with detailed comments. Some spoke to me at length via in-depth Skype and Zoom interviews. I am grateful to all of these global respondents for their valuable contributions.

Primary Challenges Holding Women Back Per Survey Responses:

What Career Challenges Are Holding You Back?

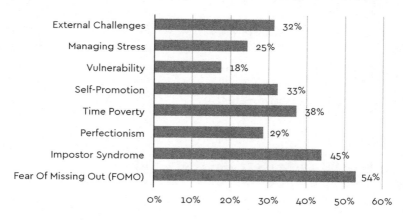

Each participant was allowed to vote/choose multiple responses

CONTENTS

INTRODUCTION

I started my career in Pakistan as a junior HR manager at the age of 22 and was promoted to senior roles within a short span of time. At a young age, I was focused on interpersonal skills. My key strengths were communicating with and relating to people with different backgrounds and personalities. It was therefore inevitable that I chose Human Resources as a specialty for my MBA. My late father, who was associated with the HR profession, was also an important influence.

At my first job, I was the only female in the department with 21 men, most of whom were twice my age. It was a difficult situation that made me extra cautious and always on guard. When I transitioned to my next job, the gender balance was similarly challenging. Even though there were more females in the department, I was the only one in Training & Development. I often found myself in a room full of middle-aged Asian men who had to be 'told' what to do, and as you can imagine that didn't go down very well with many of them. However, these experiences did teach me a great deal about working within male-dominated companies. My father and brother also proved to be valuable mentors who helped me navigate my career with confidence.

While working in the Human Resources department, I began developing training programmes for employees, with a keen interest for women leadership programmes. One major project I initiated was formally recognising International Women's Day through exclusive events for women. Most of our company initiatives – sports tournaments, in-house events and concerts – appealed more to men and were less inclusive for women. The first year's theme was Stress Management and I called the programme 'Rooh Afza', which means 'Revitalising Your Soul'. Because I strongly believe in 'edutainment', I always ensured that there was one core women-focused training topic to complement the fun activities throughout the day. International Women's Day became a very popular, signature programme for women in our organisation and we continued to run it year after year. After this early success, I started to realise my passion for these types of programmes.

Six-and-a-half years into my career and a year after marriage, we moved from Pakistan to Dubai for better job prospects. Despite being a busy mum, I did not give up my career aspirations and continued to work on a part-time basis as a consultant, recruiter and trainer. My husband played an important role in encouraging me to do this. I finally launched my very own training and HR consulting firm – ed Management Consulting. My passion for training and the desire to motivate, develop and positively influence the people around me realised its truest essence under this umbrella. I trained hundreds of working professionals from different nationalities, backgrounds and professions; from teachers to students, from corporate officers to police officials, my client base was quite diverse. Furthermore, my qualification as a professional coach and NLP practitioner gave me additional credibility to more effectively help clients address their personal and professional challenges. I continued the tradition of Women's Day celebrations and held annual events at many companies, sometimes even at beaches and parks, and trained hundreds of corporate career women.

Each year we followed different themes and taglines. Beyond Stress Management, we covered topics like Emotional Intelligence, Women in Leadership and Women Empowerment. As a trainer and coach, I loved providing value by facilitating the growth of these participants. The fantastic feedback they shared motivated me even more. Though I trained both men and women, I was most fulfilled by the women-only events and training sessions. Since Dubai comprises 85% expats, most of my corporate trainings included women from diverse nationalities.

When I moved to London nearly seven years later, I was aware that my background would be a formidable challenge to complement the difficulty of starting my business anew. As an Asian Muslim immigrant woman in a foreign land I was exposed to many limitations and prejudices. Naturally, I was hesitant and afraid. Although I was still relatively unknown in Dubai, life there was comfortable and my business was doing well. London, however, was a whole different uphill battle. I had already started from scratch when I moved from Pakistan to Dubai. And here I was yet again in a completely new region.

At the recommendation of my husband, I started blogging and podcasting. But then, I began questioning myself. What difference could I possibly make? Who will read my blogs and listen to my podcasts? Who am I to be successful?

Yet, regardless of how I felt, I decided to pursue my goals in earnest. Being zero tech savvy and with fear in my heart, I began my journey. I realised I would never really know how much I could accomplish unless I tried. So, try I did. I even made a commitment to myself: if just one person reads my blog or hears my podcast and benefits from it, it would be worth it.

Fast forward 24 months and I am thrilled I didn't give up during those difficult years. Thousands of people now read my blogs and I was published more than 25 times last year alone. Many of my articles were shared by leading podcasters and bloggers – even Arianna Huffington herself. I look back at my own accomplishments with profound gratitude. One of the most important lessons I learned was to never stop believing in myself. If you do come across self-doubt, just ask yourself this: *Who am I not to be successful?*

Contrary to what I believed, London was more open-minded than I expected; I quickly forged lasting business and professional friendships. I had been coaching in Asia and the Middle East for more than a decade, but online media enabled me to extend my global reach to women in Europe, the US, Canada, Nigeria and Australia. Social platforms enable you to exchange valuable learnings and develop close bonds with women you may never meet in person. Training women from different regions gave me the opportunity to solicit feedback from diverse groups of women that proved to be quite beneficial for the survey that informed this book.

Much to my surprise, I discovered that even though some issues are endemic to women within certain cultures, there is sufficient evidence that many of the challenges working women face are global.

I am very grateful to all the women who have contributed to this book. Some of these respondents are women I already knew including working friends, family members and other professional contacts. The majority of the others are those I corresponded with for the first time for this survey.

CHAPTER 1:

WHAT HAPPENED ALONG THE WAY?

*Men are taught to apologise for their
weaknesses, women for their strengths.*

Lois Wyse

Recently I have been part of many initiatives that seek to mentor young girls in schools and colleges. Last year, I supported a teen girl conference attended by more than 200 teenage girls from schools across London. The most striking characteristic these girls shared was their unswerving confidence. These girls were asking thoughtful questions – carefully crafted and coherently delivered – with uninhibited courage. Some were poised enough to conduct on-camera interviews. Several of them had their future plans mapped out, and they communicated those goals to the rest of the audience in a very self-assured manner. They were already confident, eloquent and knowledgeable.

I couldn't help but wonder if these girls would manifest the same undeterred courage as they grow up. What if they lose that courage and confidence? That sobering thought made me think about all the revealing surveys which indicate just how much confidence girls shed as they mature.

A *Girl Guiding* study recently found that while 63% of seven- to ten-year-old girls feel confident in themselves, only 31% of 17- to

21-year-olds feel that way. The same study also found that a mere 35% of 17- to 21-year-olds believed they had an equal chance of succeeding compared to their male colleagues, whereas 90% of nine- and ten-year-old girls believed they did.

In 2011, the United Kingdom's Institute of Leadership and Management surveyed British managers about how confident they feel in their professions. Half the female respondents reported self-doubt about their job performance and careers, compared with less than a third of male respondents.

Professor of Economics at Carnegie Mellon University and author of *Women Don't Ask*, Linda Babcock, found in studies of business school students that men initiate salary negotiations four times as often as women do, and that when women do negotiate, they ask for 30% less money than men.

The Confidence Code reveals that at England's Manchester Business School, Professor Marilyn Davidson asks her students every year what they expect to earn, and what they deserve to earn five years after graduation. Every year there are massive differences between male and female responses to that simple question. She reports that, on average, men think they deserve £80,000 a year while women believe they are worth just £64,000 – or 20% less.

Another survey conducted by the American Association of University Women revealed that girls emerge from adolescence with a poor self-image, relatively low expectations from life and much less confidence in themselves and their abilities than boys do. Furthermore, the study identified adolescence as the moment when girls begin to doubt themselves: while 11-year-olds tend to be full of self-confidence, by 15 and 16 they start to say: "I don't know, I don't know, I don't know."

But then if young girls are confident until the age of 13, *what exactly happens after adolescence that leads to this drop in confidence?* Does a gendered upbringing along with cultural conditioning, schooling, and a girl's own growing awareness of sexism have a role to play in this?

Confidence in boys largely remains unfazed as they progress into manhood. However, as girls mature, their need to belong intensifies, and they often adjust their ambitions, and even attempt to tame their confidence, so others don't form negative opinions about them. And since girls want to be liked and crave approval, they ditch the strong and rebellious elements of their personality to avoid appearing too bossy or overconfident.

Society rewards girls for being 'good' not audacious. Society rewards them for being cooperative and compliant and not impudent. So there's little surprise that's exactly what they do: 'put their heads down and play by the rules'. This societal gender imbalance makes confidence a conundrum and gives rise to faulty confidence meters, which later impacts their professional lives too.

Hence, we can't deny that most of us are products of gendered upbringing and cultures. There are social realities that compound female self-doubt – after all, the one situation we can never avoid is our gender. That's precisely why most of our internal challenges like Impostor Syndrome, Fear Of Missing Out, Perfectionism, etc. have a deeper social context.

Many times, we remain blocked by invisible barriers despite our best efforts. That's when we need to contextualise the blocks we face in our careers and identify whether it's us or the people and environment around us. It's worth considering if it is time to move on and focus our energy elsewhere.

Males often consider themselves more knowledgeable and secure than women. And why wouldn't they? After all, this world attributes a man's success to his ability, but a woman's success is often attributed to good timing, luck or 100 other factors other than her own accomplishments. Conversely, failures in a man's world can be bad luck while failure in a woman's world is due to lack of preparation or a subpar skillset.

As quoted in *The Confidence Code*, Lindsay Hudson, Chief Executive Officer of BAE Systems, notes: "When a man walks in the room, they are assumed to be competent until they prove otherwise. For women it's the other way round."

Making matters worse, women tend to linger over failures, or even the thought of failing, much longer than men do. Men on the other hand let tough remarks and failures slide off their back much more easily. As Michelle Obama recently said: "I wish that girls could fail as well as men do and be OK. Because let me tell you, watching men fail up, it's frustrating. It's frustrating to see men blow it and win. And we hold ourselves to these crazy, crazy standards."

Brené Brown has made a name for herself via her ongoing TEDx talks on vulnerability and her leadership books. She speaks about Mahalik's Boston College research in one of her talks. When she asked: "What do women need to do to conform to female norms?" the top answers in the United States are: "be nice; be thin; be modest; and use all available resources for appearance." When she asked: "What do men in this country need to do to conform to male norms?" the answers were vastly different: "always show emotional control; put work first; pursue status; and violence." This in itself reflects the stereotypes associated with women.

Historically, women have had to work twice as hard. As Swedish immunologists Christine Wenneras and Agnes Wold discovered, women scientists have had to be 2.5 times more productive as men to be judged equal. No wonder women hold themselves to higher standards!

In *Lean In*, Sandberg emphasises the importance of raising your hand and keeping it raised. She confesses to having ignored a woman in the group in preference to a man simply because the woman didn't raise her hand long enough to get attention.

I keep telling my clients that opportunities come to those who have the courage to step up and ask. But that's not where your role ends. It's equally important to not back down once you have asked a question or spoken up. Women are taught to be polite and diplomatic, to not raise their voice or act boastful. As women, we are accustomed to traditional female modes of communication which often underpin compliance and modesty. *Don't be too loud. Wait for your turn. Don't interrupt. Let the other person finish. Don't be pushy. Don't brag.*

Soccer star Abby Wambach's Barnard Commencement Address is one of the best speeches I have heard lately. Here is what she says: "Like all little girls, I was taught to be grateful. I was taught to keep my head down, stay on the path, and get my job done. I was freaking Little Red Riding Hood," Wambach said, referencing the lessons of the fairy tale. "The message is clear: Don't be curious, don't make trouble, don't say too much, or bad things will happen. I stayed on the path out of fear – not of being eaten by a wolf – but of being cut, being benched, losing my paycheck. If I could go back and tell my younger self one thing, it would be this: 'Abby, you were never Little Red Riding Hood, you were always the wolf.'"

Furthermore, Abby recalls the night she received her award along with two other incredible athletes. It was the same night she also realised that even though all three made the same sacrifices, shed the same amount of blood, sweat and tears, left it all on the field for decades with the same ferocity, talent and commitment, their retirements wouldn't be the same at all. The men walked away with something she didn't have: fat bank accounts. "Because of that, they had something else I didn't have: freedom. Their hustling days were over, and mine were just beginning."

The clichéd labels like 'dumb blondes', 'beauty without brains' are prevalent and very real. They have also been substantiated by women who experience these terms on a daily basis. Betty Bruen from my survey confides that one of her personal work challenges was that her male colleagues considered her stupid because she was also attractive. Betty also suffered from the inability to say no.

Moreover, success and likeability are positively co-related for men, but successful women are seen as overly ambitious, career oriented, cold, bossy, and of course the favourite 'b' word (the default label for women who dare to speak up or be different). There is a stereotypical expectation from women to be 'nice', communal and nurturing. And when they defy these expectations and reach out for opportunities just like men do, it creates dissonance in people's minds and these women are judged ill-favourably. More success leads to more vitriol not just from men but females too! Many women who have reached the pinnacle have reported unspoken waves of prejudice. As they say: "Damned if you do and damned if you don't."

Rene Ugarte noted that her personal challenge is continually failing to be the 'right' kind of woman and being unapologetic about it. The McKinsey study further supports that men are promoted based on potential while women are promoted based on past accomplishments. No wonder we are so hung up on what we deserve and what we don't. Did anyone say impostor?

To avoid detection and shield ourselves from insecurity, we make extraordinary efforts to mask our supposed ineptness. We obsess over every minute detail, studying exhaustively, staying up that much later, studying even harder, doing and redoing tasks ad nauseam. Hello perfectionists, I hear you!

In order to protect ourselves from being liked, we question our abilities and downplay our achievements, especially in the presence of others. We put ourselves down before others can. When you choose to hold back your successes and downplay your achievements instead, I know where you are coming from! Modesty, thy name is women, or was it frailty?

As women, the world shames us if our homes and children show even the slightest sign of neglect. When you feel exhausted and overwhelmed, or fear missing out on any of the many roles you juggle daily, there is often an underlining societal pressure at play.

As much as we all loved the film *Bad Moms*, no one would really aspire to be a bad mother in real life, would they? So we work hard, constantly multitask and try to make the best of every role and responsibility entrusted to us to overcome what Sandberg calls 'the holy trinity of fear': fear of being a bad mother, bad wife or bad daughter. To top that, professional penalties for men and women are quite different. For example, women are more harshly judged for their appearance and choice of attire than men. Obesity is known to have a more demoralising impact on working women than working men.

Heather from my survey shares that she is most impacted by lack of equality outside the workplace. She struggled with feelings of inadequacy, as though she would be judged if her kids' clothes were creased, the house wasn't spotless, etc. She also struggled with the sole responsibility of managing the family childcare they outsource and has always been resentful that this reflects poorly on her (ie the school always calls her and not her husband, etc).

What's worse, some of us even procrastinate and dabble before reaching the finish line for fear of being criticised or to avoid the shame of not making it. We are scared to be vulnerable and admit our mistakes as well as our shortcomings. The vulnerability we could use to our advantage becomes our very undoing. And when we do experience failures, we internalise them. If only we could internalise our successes just as well.

And if that wasn't enough, we have very real challenges to contend with such as lack of infrastructure and childcare options, flexi-timing, misogynistic work environments and sexual harassment.

A recent campaign by the UK Mayor of London's office showed a video shot at an underground station in which men were asked to take the escalator and women were asked to take the stairs. The video also revealed a shocking discovery: "A CEO is more likely to be called John than be a woman." The concept execution was noteworthy as it conveyed a key point and highlighted how the path to leadership is too slow for women. The escalator signified the privilege men have as compared to women who have traditionally taken the longer, harder route and highlighted the disparity of opportunity. I was a little disappointed to see that not a single woman raised an objection on being asked to take the stairs instead of the lift.

None of the men stopped to enquire when prompted to take the lift versus the stairs. It suggested that men are more focused on their own personal journeys versus considering those of their female counterparts.

The video also showed a woman taking the stairs with a pram. To me, the woman with a pram reflected the extra 'motherhood penalty' many mums have to pay to pursue their career. Clearly society applies different rules to benefit men over women. The video also suggested women are submissive and willing to blindly follow authority despite personal struggle.

Several women from my own survey attested to the social conditioning and differences they experience as compared to their male counterparts. Many women have also talked about what is commonly called the 'gender discount'. Alison said that she is still questioned whether she qualifies for a job because she only has an Associate's Degree in Liberal Arts even though she has years of on-the-job experience. My response to that is: "Would the situation be different if she was Adam?" Why do women need to demonstrate their worth via additional degrees and qualifications when most men are comfortable just the way they are?

Jana who was quoted earlier too, admitted: "Before I went to therapy I often thought, when encountering misogyny, that it was my fault for falling short as a person (sometimes it was, but not always). Sometimes it was a man assuming he was entitled to treat me as a second-class person. The most galling part about it is that many of them don't even know there is a problem because they are stuck way past their eyeballs in white male privilege. But regardless of having your own house in order, if one encounters overt misogyny it should be called out."

Jeanine said her main challenge at work is the inability to recognise her own worth and success; she constantly focuses on where she could improve, completely missing the fact that she is already surpassing all of her peers in performance. "How can we learn how to judge ourselves objectively, so we can recognise when our superiors are not doing so?" she asks. Although Jeanine does not feel like a fraud or an impostor, she does feel that the expectations others have for her are much greater – almost unattainable – when compared to her peers. "No matter what I achieve I'll always be 'the woman' and therefore not seen as promotable past a certain point. When I forget this, I internalise and start focusing on what I could be doing better. But I need to recognise the disparate treatment. Women just accept they aren't good enough without looking at the actual facts/numbers."

Anne added that one challenge women constantly face is that they sabotage themselves out of fear of success – fear of the onslaught of assumptions and criticisms that go with being a successful woman.

I couldn't agree more with Anne. Not only are women scared of failure, but they are also scared of success. They are scared to be called overambitious or selfish – labels that are generally associated with successful women. As Sheryl Sandberg says: "Fear is the root of so many barriers women face. Fear of not being liked. Fear of making the wrong choice. Fear of drawing negative attention. Fear of overreaching. Fear of being judged. Fear of failure."

I remember a few months back, my friend and money mind expert Gull Khan was conducting a financial manifestation class. In that class, she asked us to write down our dream income. Many of us, including myself, hesitated to pen this down. In the next exercise, she asked us to double the income. And that's when almost all of us became terrified and uncomfortable. When she started exploring as to why we were uncomfortable, it turns out it wasn't because we thought the income was unattainable or overambitious but we were scared to confront the changes that will come along with it. Most feared that they might not be able to justify time and commitment to their family once they started earning that much. Some were nervous about family reactions. Some even deliberated if their husband will be comfortable if they started earning twice as much. And then there were others who thought that their 'niceness', or perhaps the perception of it, might be impacted if they started earning a lot.

You see, that's what social conditioning does to you. All these examples are clear evidence that in reality women face a combination of both internal and external challenges that make this ceiling thicker than it looks. Unless we address both sets of challenges, we won't be able to break through this ceiling as often as we'd like.

KT Ellis pointed out that many of the challenges included in my survey are also traits that gifted people have, especially gifted women who are made to feel guilty for either using their intelligence and ignoring their personal lives, or ignoring their intelligence in favour of starting a family. She feels in both ways 'women can't win'.

Hence, there is a very good reason why most challenges are labelled gender specific. After all, gender does play a role in making you feel less competent than you really are, and making your job much tougher than it is. Somewhere along the way between the classroom and the cubicle the rules change, and girls are thrust into a work environment that no longer rewards them for exemplary behaviour. As a result, their confidence takes a beating and the otherwise self-confident 13-year-old eventually gives way to a new, hesitant, unsure woman who thinks twice before stepping up or owning her success.

Women In Minority

Being a woman is already tough, but being a minority woman is even tougher. Among women who already fare worse than men in terms of seniority level, minority women are most rare, says Georgene Huang, founder of *FairyGodBoss* and a *Women@ Forbes* contributor.

Compared to most women, minority women face far greater challenges in their careers, including isolation, discrimination, and low self-esteem. Being in double minority means twice the road blocks!

Cherron Inko Tarriah, a powerful black woman and founder of Staff Networks, shared a heart-wrenching narrative with me about her experience as a minority woman. Cherron held highly esteemed professional roles and had an excellent track record leading multi-million pound policies and yet...

> *"I was seen as 'a safe pair of hands' but never 'strategic', 'analytical' or 'a leader'. I watched colleagues who achieved less go further. It was easier for them somehow. My mind was telling me that because of how I looked, I'm not supposed to do this or do that and so I accepted it when they told me that I wasn't quite ready for promotion, despite the fact that I was doing work beyond my pay grade. I believed it (for years) because of words spoken to me (or about people like me) or things that I've experienced.*
>
> *For example, as a HR manager, I often chaired interview panels. On more than one occasion, I would be asked if I was on the panel to take the notes. Or when I was in a meeting and asked pertinent questions, colleagues would often address their answers to my (white male) colleague - completely avoiding any eye contact with me. Or despite being in businesswear, I would be mistaken for a cleaner! These daily micro assaults and micro aggressions slowly eroded my confidence.*
>
> *I started to believe that I was deficient in some way. And when I did pluck up the courage and decided to challenge comments, I was told:*

'You're so sensitive'; 'They were only having a laugh'; 'Don't be so touchy.' There was a battle going on in my mind. On the one hand, I knew I was ambitious, passionate and competent, but this dark, ugly emotion called fear kept hanging around causing mayhem in my mind. It's that little voice that says: 'Don't get ideas above yourself,' or 'Just stay in your comfort zone,' or 'What makes you so special?' or 'You don't want to be seen as a troublemaker,' or 'You'll fall flat on your face like so and so.' And so you retreat. As I did for many years. I hid my strengths and underplayed my value."

Cherron's experience echoes that of thousands of minority women who have had similar or worse experiences in which the system 'dictates their potential and sucks out their confidence and self-doubt'. While Cherron was confident enough to overcome her fear and take that leap of faith, there are hundreds of others who are silently enduring every day.

As I was finishing the first draft of this book, I came across an appalling piece of news which momentarily made me want to shut down this project entirely. A report on gender balance detailed ten ridiculous reasons for not appointing women to FTSE (Financial Times and Stock Exchange) company boards. Women don't fit in, don't want the hassle, and struggle with 'complex issues' were some of the excuses used.

A few weeks back, I was already quite perturbed to hear an excuse made by an event organiser back home to justify why women weren't invited to conferences there. According to him these conferences are gender exclusive by design. My response to that: there is no such thing as 'gender exclusive by design'. Designs are meant to be improved and evolved with time, otherwise we would still be using mainframe computers and cassette players.

Countries in South Asia rank low in terms of gender equality, but in all fairness, these countries also face a myriad of other challenges typically shared by developing countries. Women's representation is not really the top agenda item in these regions, so misogynist excuses for lack of female representation on boards or at conferences often don't come as a surprise.

But when an advanced and developed country comes up with this list, it gives me cause for concern. Are we really living in 2018 or have we travelled back to the prehistoric age? Amanda Mackenzie very rightly calls this 'a script from the comedy parody' and states that this script looks like it's from 1918. If such outdated and senseless excuses are given in the 21st century, what hope do we have?

As I was sipping hot chocolate, silently fuming over this latest report and flicking channels aimlessly, I came across a news brief which stopped me short. Two women with their heads and faces covered were giving an on-camera interview to a local TV channel. These women belonged to KPK in Pakistan, an area previously occupied by terrorists. As I heard them speak, I was awestruck. These women weren't any ordinary women. They were bomb disposal officers. Woah! I hadn't come across many female bomb disposal squads before, let alone in my own country. My heart soared with pride.

These women shared how their father wanted them to be on a par with men in their community. Their covered faces and heads evidenced respect for cultural norms, yet they made an unusual career choice – choosing to risk their lives for a job few men would dare pursue. They said they did not want to feel that daughters were a burden on the family. Women in the province are usually considered 'unfit' for difficult jobs like disposing of explosives in a terrorism-affected province. However, here they were, defying all odds to prove their mettle in the field. I later found out that these women weren't the only ones.

There were others too. I then thought of Malala, Pakistani activist for female education, and the late Benazir Bhutto, the first female prime minister of Pakistan. Despite being brought up in a misogynist environment in which bold women aren't always looked upon kindly, these women had managed to smash all barriers and make a difference, rising above all stereotypes and biases. What can we learn from these women? Obviously, they were not letting external challenges impact them. They had likely mastered their internal challenges first to find the courage to do what they did every single day.

In the article *Men Aren't Holding Us Back – We're Doing It Ourselves*, author Liz Jones recognises that: "It isn't men who need to change in order for us to get to the top. It's us. The reason women aren't on the board is not the fault of men. It's our fault. We simply conduct business in a different way. We don't always think we are right. We scare (quite easily in my case). We protect subordinates. We are not arrogant, have children and lives and housework, but we also have empathy. We see the person, not the job title."

And that's precisely why it is crucial to rise above our internal challenges before we step up and fight the external ones; as one of my survey respondents aptly said: "We need to get our own house in order first."

INTERNAL CHALLENGES

Yesterday I was clever, so I wanted to change the world.
Today I am wise so I want to change myself.

Rumi

CHAPTER 2:

THE FEAR OF MISSING OUT [FOMO]

FOMO lures us out of our integrity with whispers about what we could or should be doing. FOMO's favourite weapon is comparison. It kills gratitude and replaces it with 'not enough'. We answer FOMO's call by saying YES when we mean NO. We abandon our path and our boundaries and those precious adventures that hold meaning for us so that we can prove that we aren't missing out!

Brené Brown

Fear Of Missing Out

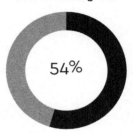

54%

Ladies and gentlemen, we have a winner! A majority of the 300 working women from across the globe revealed that the primary challenge holding them back is the Fear Of Missing Out. It's important to note that most of the women respondents were working mums, though women without children reported it too.

Fear Of Missing Out, or FOMO for short, was added to the Oxford English Dictionary in 2013. It is the most common fear impacting women today. Recent studies have shown that FOMO is often linked to feelings of disconnection and dissatisfaction, and social media only fuels it. Think of how many people constantly scan Facebook or Instagram to keep up with friends' perfect 'Instagram moments'. Some people don't just want to keep up – they start comparing and evaluating their lives based on how they see others portraying theirs.

Clinical psychologist Anita Sanz reveals scientific data in this regard and how a part of our brain is specialised for sensing 'being left out'. This part of the brain is a component of the limbic system, the amygdala, whose job it is to detect whether something could be a threat to our survival. Not having vital information, or getting the impression that one is not a part of the 'in' group, is enough for many amygdalas to engage the stress or activation response commonly known as the 'fight or flight' response. In an attempt to avoid additional stress, some people will (unfortunately) redouble their efforts to not miss out on anything and end up in an almost constant process of 'checking' behaviour.

A large majority of women in my survey have experienced Fear Of Missing Out across the various roles they play. Not surprisingly, the most notable FOMO role is that of mother. As Arianna Huffington points out: "I think while all mothers deal with feelings of guilt, working mothers are plagued by guilt on steroids."

Was I surprised? No. As a mum myself, I know that 'mum guilt' is an undeniable, powerful feeling that affects the majority of working mums and even stay-at-home mums too. While it's normal for both men and women to feel anticipatory regret from time to time, FOMO mums lose perspective and often make decisions they don't want to make. A friend of mine told me that whether or not she is making the right choices for her children is a question that crosses her mind at least once a day! And she is not alone. Working mums are often consumed with the pervasive underlying concern of whether they are making the right choices or missing out on something.

The first few years of my career I took a break from working full time and only picked up freelance assignments. Eventually, I launched my own business. Even though I had a nanny back in Dubai, I was hesitant to leave my son behind and constantly feared missing out, one way or another.

Here's the thing, a mother's guilt is forever... as in I should have done this, and I should have done that. Those persistent thoughts will always be there. But what exactly is mum guilt? It's that nagging feeling that you aren't doing enough for your children. Working mums have it even tougher as society often judges them based on the so-called 'abandonment' of children. This mum guilt inevitably leads to Fear Of Missing Out because you are constantly under pressure, worrying about the duties, the fun, the responsibilities that are an integral part of being a perfect mum, professional etc. When at work, you fear missing out on the time you could have spent with your children, partner, family, etc. When you are at home or leave early, you constantly feel guilty and fear that you are missing out on important assignments at work. So as women, we are never really secure in our decisions and thus we enter a vicious cycle of guilt and self-doubt.

In her article *The Heartbreaking Way FOMO Fuels Working Mum Guilt*, Sara defines this guilt and says: "It is the feeling that I am missing out on the magic of seeing my beautiful little girl blossom into the person she is going to become. The sense that miracles happen in the ordinary and our ordinary is relegated to a few hours in the evening during the week and the weekends."

In my survey, Charla confesses that Fear Of Missing Out has been her primary challenge at work. She feels guilty that her son is in daycare all day and she can't pick him up earlier to spend time with him and teach him things.

Deb, a US-based Canadian, agrees that FOMO is definitely her biggest challenge at work. She even took her $3\frac{1}{2}$-month-old son to Egypt on an archaeological project!

Naomi admits that FOMO is also her worst challenge. She felt like a self-described 'shitty' mum when she left on a business trip and missed the first two nights of Chanukkah. Sometimes when she is with her kids but needs to get a proposal to a client she feels like she can't be fully present. "It SUCKS!" she adds, exasperated.

Tai revealed that she travels extensively as well. "Last night my kiddo and I lit the first candle (electric) of Chanukkah together on FaceTime... it was kind of magical! But, yes, it's tough", she adds.

In the article *Why Motherhood Needs to be More Compatible With Having a Career,* author Sarah Biddlecombe writes: "I used to love hearing from my babysitter what the kids had been up to all day, but I found myself wishing I could see for myself."

As a working mum, the stress remains almost perpetually. Much of the stress is because there aren't enough hours in the day to fully dedicate to either work or family. In her book *Lean In*, Sheryl Sandberg recommends finding a partner who can help, but in reality, such a find is often rare and, moreover, many women are single mums.

A National Parenting Association survey found that although 86% of women graduating from college reported wanting to have children, close to half of them were still childless by age 40. Compare these figures to the 79% of men in the survey who indicated they wanted children and the 75% who later had children. It becomes rather obvious that while career men don't generally experience a gap between what they want and what they get (at least with respect to children), career women do.

In another article, *Motherhood versus Career, The Epic Battle That Need Not Be*, Sherrie Bourg Carter wrote: "Many women who work outside the home feel trapped in an impossible catch-22." She says that although these women may enjoy the independence and sense of accomplishment a job can provide, they feel guilty for leaving their children in the care of someone else during the work day. This same guilt is often experienced by women who were formerly stay-at-home mums but had to rejoin the workforce owing to financial necessity. Single career mums fall into the same category – they have to work in order to meet survival needs.

Kate, one survey respondent, says that she feels fear and anxiety about whether she is a good mum, boss and employee. She says: "I feel like men don't worry about it that much (maybe they do but it doesn't seem like it), and that then holds me back – still working on how to overcome fears."

Kim tells me that as a single working mum her main fear is missing out on being a mum, not having enough time to keep a clean house, cook good food, help with homework, etc.

After all, one person being everything for everyone is an impossible task. I distinctly remember crying after being late to my son's football award ceremony because my training session ran long. I was horrified and broken. No more work, I told myself. I had opted out of a full-time job and started my own business so that I could enjoy these little moments! What's the point if I am still missing them? Out of guilt and fear that this trend might continue, I said no to a project the very next day. Many women cannot pursue travelling assignments or long work days due to the same fear, but those that do, suffer nevertheless. Even if they want to travel by choice, they are usually not selected for such trips as it's automatically assumed they wouldn't want to.

Saamia says that for a lot of girls in Pakistan or other Asian countries it's FOMO that wears them out, especially when there are people around them who constantly remind them how perfect their parenting skills are and how 'on top of everything' they are. "But deep down you know they say a lot of stuff to make you feel bad. It really helps if you have a supportive husband," she adds.

Lailumah agrees there is no FOMO if there is a solid support system. One only has to prove herself when there is a poor system and lack of confidence.

Khalida confides her top challenge is FOMO and it has nothing to do with confidence. "But in your surroundings, you are constantly reminded that you are not capable or perfect."

FOMO like many other internal challenges is culturally influenced. Women especially typically feel this fear because of societal obligations traditionally passed on to them and the judgments they are subjected to if they neglect any of these obligations or responsibilities. Asian mothers were more affected by FOMO than any other challenge. This is not surprising considering how working mothers are largely looked down upon in that culture; women are expected to stay at home and maintain the family as their first priority.

Some countries exhibit a progressive and practical attitude. For example, Katinka Barysch's research article showed that almost two-thirds of British men would be happy to stay at home and look after the kids if their wife was earning enough. In Asia, such an arrangement is considered taboo.

According to a report by UNDP, United Nation's Development Programme, the gender difference in Pakistan can be expressed as the inside/outside dichotomy: women are mostly exposed to inner household boundaries and are thus restricted to the duties of keeping the house in order. "Their contributions to raising the family and farm affairs are considered their cultural duty and gender-specific role."

In a group discussion with Sarah and Amnah from the Middle East, the latter expressed their frustration with the double standards working mothers are subjected to. Often these women have had to forego work trips for fear of being judged for leaving their kids on their own (even though 'on their own' meant leaving them with their dad and a house full of grandparents, uncles and aunts all living together).

Working mothers experience this same pressure in some European countries. For example, in Germany, studies show that people believe mothers should stay at home (note that not all studies are directly comparable to my own). Just one in five Germans believes that mothers of young children should work full time. Only 40% of men say they would accept a setback in their own career to allow their wives to get ahead. And German women agree: fewer than half want to see a change in the prevalent division of gender roles.

The biggest difference observed is in public attitudes. In Britain, the question of whether and how much a mother should work is seen as a matter of either necessity or personal preference. In Germany, the debate has a moralising, sometimes even antagonistic, tone.

Despite the fact that we live in a more progressive and equal global society than ever before, women around the world still tend to do the lion's share of the work, from taking care of the household to looking after children to maintaining familial ties; the workload doesn't decrease for working women who face the quintessential double bind.

A National Parenting Association survey found that successful working women are much more likely to assume primary responsibility for their homes and children than their husbands or partners. The survey detailed that 50% of successful married women are primarily responsible for meal preparation (compared to only 9% of their husbands), and 51% take time off from work to care for a sick child (compared to only 9% percent of their husbands).

"We tend to talk more about inequality in the workplace, and yet the inequality in the home is really stuck," says Kathleen L. McGinn, Cahners-Rabb Professor of Business Administration at Harvard Business School. McGinn was part of a research study that revealed employed women from developed countries spend twice as much time as men doing household work and caring for the family. Also, remember the mum Heather from my previous chapter who believed that it was always her fault whenever clothes were creased or the home wasn't spotless?

Despite being in the 21st century, there is an absence of support to assist working mothers who wish to transition back into a career following childbirth. Maternity leave and pay conditions are much less flexible in the UK than in other European countries like Germany. That's why most UK mums are back at work six to nine months after giving birth. Moreover, UK positions are usually kept open for one year versus other European cities where mums have the right to return to their previous jobs up to three years after giving birth. In addition, quality childcare is so expensive that many European and British mums opt to stay at home even though the majority of British women say they would like to combine a career with having a family if possible.

Other Types Of FOMO

For mums, it's not just about fear of what they are missing by choosing career over their children or vice versa; many mums have a major FOMO for their kids. These mums will sign up for every extra-curricular activity and every play date that comes their way. Mummy blogger Sarah writes: "I don't know if that has to do more with parenting itself, or the fact that we are privy to everyone else's style of parenting. But whatever the reason is, you end up running round in circles trying to make sure your kid is never missing out on anything. You line up endless play dates, attend birthdays every weekend, sign her up for different after-school activities and basically make your car your second home." She ends up saying yes to more plans for her children than for herself. Sarah admits that there is "exhaustion in running the FOMO race" and she often finds herself wishing that they weren't so busy.

But it's important to know FOMO exists in non-mums too. Moreover, women experience different types of FOMO. An article from *Psychologies Magazine* points out: "FOMO is a phenomenon that predates the trendy abbreviation; it's a modern take on the grass being greener on the other side."

Even if you don't have children, women still need to return to their parents, partners, siblings, pets and friends – the guilt of choosing work over these relationships is the same. At work, women face the Fear Of Missing Out on assignments or project details. To address this fear, you say yes to everything, exhausting yourself with every detail and ultimately getting overwhelmed by the myriad of tasks you've taken on. For example, when I was writing this book, I made it a point to read as many articles and books as I could so that I didn't miss out on any important information that could support my observations. As a result, I ended up with more than 100 pages of reference content. Needless to say, I made that much more work for myself because I then had to edit that wealth of content down into a more palatable length.

The biggest danger of FOMO is that it saps time. Rather than actually maximising time by accomplishing something, people spend time worrying about what they're not accomplishing. Ironically, they become so terrified of what they're missing that they end up missing things anyway. As Perri Lewis from *Psychologies Magazine* notes: people suffering from FOMO always say yes to invitations, have three screens open on their laptop at once, run multiple projects simultaneously and generally find themselves always 'on'.

Sometimes, it's not about how well you are doing something or whether you are devoting enough time to it; sometimes it's about how fast you have reached a goal in life, especially when it comes to getting married or family planning. Even today, woman are scrutinised if they choose not to have children. They often face criticism, and as their biological clock ticks, it adds more stress.

A woman's decision to not have children is inextricably linked to pursuing a career, a fact which triggers a barrage of labels such as 'selfish', 'power hungry', 'greedy', and self-centred'. These women are constantly reminded that the path they chose does not meet society's expectations for them.

Having just turned 30, Tiffany believes there is a stigma associated with aging: once women are out of their 20s, they are past their prime. She confides: "I still don't know if I want kids, and the window for that is closing. But I'm not going to rush it. I also feel a little bit like I have to hurry and get 'successful' really fast, because I got a later start in my career. I was a high school and college dropout who got divorced at 20."

These FOMO issues are addressed in more detail within the Time Management chapter.

Coping Strategies For FOMO

Accept That It's OK To Not Have It All At The Same Time

The very first thing you need to understand is that 'having it all' has a lot to do with your perception and relevant needs. Some women feel that juggling responsibilities causes them to lose a few hours here and there and they are thus missing out on one thing or another. Others may see this trade-off as necessary and understand that they do have everything despite that.

The second thing you should know is that if you do miss out, it's OK to not have everything given trade-offs are inevitable. You will make sacrifices and compromises, so be crystal clear with yourself about why you are making those trade-offs as this clarity is essential to stave off future guilt.

I, for one, truly believe that women can be whatever they want to be and have everything they want. However, that doesn't mean women can have everything at the exact same time. "We *can't* have it all," recognises former *Vogue* editor-in-chief Alexandra Shulman who also believes women are setting 'impossible standards' for themselves. Despite being an obvious champion of ambitious women, she doesn't believe that women can 'have it all'.

In Douglas Rushkoff's blog *No, We Can't Have It All*, he suggests that: "We must abandon the notion that anyone – man or woman – can fully dedicate themselves to both family and career at the same time. Sadly, perhaps, one parent will end up doing more parenting and miss out on career opportunities, while the other will miss out on some family joys but end up higher on the corporate ladder. This is more the problem of competitive corporate culture than it is the failure of individuals to find balance or to work hard enough."

Businesswoman and author of *Girl Boss*, Sophia Amoruso, writes this: "It has been said that you can't have it all, but I call bulls… on that. We can have it all. Just not all at the same time."

PepsiCo CEO Indra Nooyi, who is a very powerful corporate career woman, also believes that women can't have it all. "We pretend we have it all. We pretend we can have it all. My husband and I have been married for 34 years and we have two daughters. Every day you have to make a decision about whether you are going to be a wife or a mother, in fact many times during the day you have to make those decisions. And you have to co-opt a lot of people to help you. We co-opted our families to help us." She adds.

In the same interview, she further recalls the day she was asked to be President of the Board of Directors – a monumental achievement but when she excitedly arrived home to share the news with family, her mom immediately told her to get a bottle of milk and asked her to share the news later. Here is what her mom said: "You might be president of PepsiCo. You might be on the board of directors. But when you enter this house, you're the wife, you're the daughter, you're the daughter-in-law, you're the mother. You're all of that. Nobody else can take that place. So leave that damned crown in the garage. And don't bring it into the house. You know I've never seen that crown."

In her LinkedIn blog Katya Anderson discusses her cousin's novel *The Glitch*. It's the story of Shelley Stone, a wife, mother, and tech company CEO who is committed to living her most efficient life. To have it all, she takes her 'me time' at 3.30am on the treadmill, swallows Dramamine so she can work in the car, and buys a men's multivitamin because she refuses to participate in her own oppression. The novel spans genres as part satire, part sci-fi and part mystery. Katya further adds that for them it's less about 'having it all' and more about finding the best way to 'keep it all together'. In the blog she also interviews the author Elizabeth Cohen who says it's not easy: "I wanted to write a story that was honest about the contradictions that working mothers face: to clock long hours at work but also be a devoted, hands-on mum; to prioritise family but in a way that never interferes with a meeting or work event; to be strong and aggressive but come across as pleasant and 'nice'; to be attractive but also smart; to have gravitas yet not look old."

Elizabeth further adds that she has never worked harder than she did as a working mum. No matter how much effort she puts in, she often feels like she is 'coming up short', by short-changing her kids, her job or herself. She confesses that some people perform really well under pressure and being bound to a tight schedule, but she wants to be occasionally sick and take a day off – a concept that is often not on the cards for working mums. Those mums who do work extra hard wake up super early or forgo 'me time' after work. Elizabeth adds that working dads don't feel the same pressures since they are not responsible for housework nor burdened by society's expectations. When talking about her husband she observes he has the ability to tune out certain things: "He doesn't read all the emails from school, and he doesn't feel bad about that. I feel an obligation to read them all."

This was so relatable!

The above examples put everything in a realistic perspective. If we keep believing in the idealistic notion that as women we can and must strive to have everything – a shining career, a blossoming family life and a perfectly balanced lifestyle all at once – then we are placing unrealistic expectations on ourselves. These impractical fantasies make millions of women blame themselves if they cannot climb the corporate ladder as fast as men, maintain a family and healthy home life, and be thin and beautiful as well. But the truth is you will always be missing out on something and that's OK. No one can have it all. Not even men.

There is a time for everything. If my career is doing exceptionally well right now, that's because my son is older, and busy with school and after-school activities. A few years ago this was not the case. Despite employing a full-time nanny, I did not have the luxury of free time so my career took a back seat to motherhood. Having said that, I know there are professional mothers doing an amazing job managing both work and family lives. But these 'supermums' have either one or several of the following remarkable advantages: they are incredibly organised; self-employed; work from home or have flex hours at work; and/or have a solid support network with a dedicated spouse/partner and extended family.

Jane from London says: "For me, it's more NOMO (necessity of missing out). Full-time working, parenting and trying hard to be a good wife, friend and daughter whilst holding everything together means that some things have to give. I wish I could do it all."

Appreciate The Value Of Playgroups And Daycare

The care and education most kids in childcare centres receive is top-notch. I was primarily a stay-at-home mum yet my son joined a playgroup at 18 months. I don't regret the decision at all. I could see a marked difference in my son's confidence level. In his playgroup he socialised with other children from different backgrounds. He also participated in a variety of activities and trips that I could not offer at home. Despite being a 'Type A' mum (a concept I will discuss later in the book), I did not have the resources, knowledge or expertise to provide my son with rich sensory experiences. There are some wonderful mums who fill their child's day with a perfect blend of activities, but I was never one of them. And if you are like me, then quitting your full-time job to create perfect experiences for your children wouldn't be productive at all. Truthfully, it is more important for your kids to have these experiences than it is to have these experiences specifically with you or your spouse/partner.

Install Home Cameras

If you really want to savour these growth moments while maintaining a job, then leveraging technology can be a potential solution. You can always install cameras at home to see what your children are up to as you work.

Get Help

Alternative parenting is another option: let your spouse/partner, grandparent or friend fill in. Research shows how important a father's role is in the child's unbringing. Also, couples who share responsibilities in parenting are said to be happier. Moreover, the more people your child interacts with, the more it helps him/her build confidence. In particular, grandparents can play an important role in any child's development, though I am acutely aware that not all women can benefit from this family interaction given individual circumstances. But you should seek out the support of whoever you can count on without remorse.

Join Working Mum Networks

It's also a good idea to join networks that include people with similar interests. Laura from my survey shared that she misses having a support network to provide her with positive reinforcement and constructive feedback. Sometimes all you need is a girl gang of your own to vent to and bond with. Many others are experiencing the exact same feelings and dilemmas that you are; sometimes it's enough to know that you aren't alone.

Know That Research Is In Your Favour

The National Institute of Child Health and Human Development (NICHD) conducted a study in which they followed more than 1,000 American children over a 15-year period beginning at one month of age. The study revealed that children who had 100% maternal care (no outside childcare) didn't fare any better than children who received non-maternal care, including all forms of centre-based childcare, family-based childcare, relatives, and babysitters. This held true even for those children who started daycare as infants (before 12 months of age). In fact, children who spent time in high-quality childcare showed higher cognitive and language skills and better school readiness scores than other children, including those with stay-at-home mothers.

The study did reveal that a small percentage of children who spent long hours in childcare centres had more behavioural problems, such as fighting and temper tantrums. But researchers considered these issues normal given they were not severe and usually disappeared between third and fifth grade.

According to Michael Ungar, a well-known author of parenting books and resilience researcher, excessive amounts of time caring for children, especially during their elementary school years, could do more harm than good. He notes: "Finally, we have more proof that helicopter parenting harms kids. And we have an excuse to look after our own needs as parents just a little bit more." He also believes many of us may be overfunctioning as parents. Research reveals that the amount of time mothers or fathers spend with their children before they become teens has no significant impact on a child's social, academic or emotional performance. During the teenage years, however, more time spent by a mother, or a mother and father together, can decrease the risk that an adolescent becomes delinquent, sexually active, or abuses drugs, as the presence of parents helps children to self-regulate. As Ungar says: "A child who knows they are being monitored by those around them tends to keep their behavior a little more in check."

It's also important for guilt-ridden career mums to realise that family characteristics such as parents' educational levels, household income and home environment are more consistently associated with a child's development than whether or not that child attends daycare.

An article titled *Kids Benefit From Having A Working Mom* in *Harvard Business Review* cites research by Kathleen McGinn and colleagues which claims that working mums have healthier, more successful kids who are more independent and empowered as well as confident. Not sure if this research was done by a working mum to make other working mums feels better, but if Harvard is citing it then it must have value! Jokes aside, the same article in HBR noted that 'Adult women raised by working moms are more likely to have jobs themselves, more likely to hold supervisory responsibility at those jobs, and more likely to earn higher wages than women raised by stay-at-home mothers. Men raised by working mothers are more likely to contribute to household chores and spend more time caring for family members.'

Kathleen L. McGinn, who conducted the earlier mentioned research with Mayra Ruiz Castro, a researcher at HBS, and

Elizabeth Long Lingo, an embedded practitioner at Mt. Holyoke College, says: "There are very few things that we know of that have such a clear effect on gender inequality as being raised by a working mother."

In his article *Working Moms Have Healthier, More Successful Kids*, writer Michael Ungar believes improving household income can be more important than spending time with children. I couldn't agree more. In Dubai, I worked out of choice to make a positive impact and for my own mental sanity. In London, it was no longer a flexible choice. With a new standard of living and taxes to grapple with, my second income to support my family became essential. If it were up to him, my son would pursue an extra-curricular activity each day of the week. As much as I'd love to indulge him, that level of commitment is incredibly expensive.

Revisiting Ungar's research, additional findings reveal that the time mothers spend growing their family's income could do more for their children's psychological and academic outcomes than being at home constantly. Family income was a much bigger predictor of successful child development than the amount of time a mother spends with her child. That result holds at every socioeconomic level. The study's authors didn't conclude that rich people have healthier kids. What they did show was that in each income bracket, higher household income is related to improved child development.

Use Empowering Language

Margie Warrell is a best-selling author and international speaker. In her article *Letter To Working Mothers, Stop Feeling So Guilty*, Warrell confesses that she has unwittingly taken on a mother-load of 'good-parent' *shoulds* that her own mother never did. "Our *shoulds* are a melting pot of social expectations, family pressures, and unspoken 'rules' we often buy into without even realising it. Our *shoulds* are shaped by our environment, which has seen them skyrocket in recent decades with the rise of so-called 'parenting police' – experts that bombard us with advice on what a 'good' parent should, and should not, do."

When you become a working parent, life becomes more complex and you have less time to do it all. You have to get rid of your own limiting beliefs while dealing with other people's reactions. It's important to consider how you make internal decisions as a working parent and how you communicate those decisions. The power of language, and specifically the language of choice, is important in determining how you feel and how others perceive you. Thus you should replace negative and limiting language by the language of choice.

As an NLP practitioner, I've learned to replace my *shoulds* with more empowering words. The word 'should' reeks of a must-do obligation. Except for a few essential norms and expectations, my parents didn't follow a 'should book' either. My mother was always there for us, but I don't recollect her whipping up a new activity to entertain us every time we were bored. In fact, I don't recall ever saying 'I am bored'. We went on holidays and were part of many clubs, but mostly we were expected to entertain ourselves.

As parents, we place a lot of pressure on ourselves to deliver what is best for our children to support their development. I still do a great deal as a Type A mum, but I now understand those activities as things I enjoy doing versus things I should be doing. This change in perspective has allowed me to feel less pressure and guilt as a parent and given me the freedom to choose whatever is best for us. For example, I am one of those parents who spends a lot of time planning birthday parties and events. I used to fuss over every little detail. For years I used to think I did that to be the perfect parent. But over time I realised that I did what I did because I enjoyed doing it – it was passion versus obligation.

Learn To Let Go

"The fastest way to break the cycle of perfectionism and become a fearless mother is to give up the idea of doing it perfectly – indeed to embrace uncertainty and imperfection." – Arianna Huffington

Most women are inherently perfectionists. If our child's school project doesn't meet our own ridiculously high standards, we feel dissatisfied. I will explore the challenges perfectionism creates in an upcoming chapter, but briefly know that for your children perfectionism is an unknown dimension. Even if you are doing a good enough, but not perfect job, then typically that's all that matters to your kids, so stop being so harsh on yourself.

I remember once I had forgotten to pack my son a lunch for his field trip. I spent the entire day feeling guilty and fighting back tears. How could I commit such an atrocity? I am overwhelmed by my work and need to take a break, I thought to myself.

In reality, all I needed to do was set reminders on my phone as soon as I was aware of any school activity. Who would have thought that the solution to this 'ginormous' problem could be so simple? Needless to say, I arrived early to pick my son up from school that day and dramatically swept him up in my arms. "I am sorry," I told him. "Mama forgot." He acknowledged I had but because his friends shared their snack with him, he wasn't hungry. And that was that! I could have left it there but mum guilt can be pervasive. I repeatedly brought up my own forgetfulness and how he felt about it.

By the third time, my six-year-old had had enough. He firmly looked in my eyes and said: "Mama, you know what? It's OK you forgot. It happens. Please relax! You are the best mum ever!" With that he gave me a tiny kiss on my forehead and sped away. That day I learned an important lesson from my son. We as parents, and especially as mums, really do need to relax! We're human. We forget stuff. But that doesn't make us bad parents.

There is no right way when it comes to bringing up children. I am a strong advocate of the saying, 'To each their own'. The vast majority of professional mothers work incredibly hard to be the best parent they can possibly be, and that deserves encouragement, appreciation and support.

Don't Give In To Guilt

We also need to stop buying into guilt-mongers. Margie recognises that some women thrive on critiquing other women's proficiency as parents. "While you can't always avoid the righteous parenting police, you can choose to see their self-inflating opinions – on everything from disposable nappies to disciplinary tactics – for what they are: an easy way to justify their own choices and conceal doubt about their own parenting skills."

Many women work out of financial or self-actualisation necessity. Even when I didn't need the income, I still wanted to work as I needed the personal outlet. To be a good mum, you need to be in the right frame of mind. For many women, that frame of mind naturally exists, and they reconcile it by staying at home and running the household. That's their choice which I fully respect; in fact I admire the sacrifice they make.

But there are other mums who need a creative outlet and are driven to make an impact. Whether they need to or not, working is the best option for them. When you combine motherhood with a career there will always be trade-offs, sacrifices and compromises. It is crucial for your peace of mind to reconcile those trade-offs and be crystal clear with yourself about your own choices. Is it money, satisfaction, sanity? Whatever it is, know your reasons and preferences. Focus on the benefits of the choices you make. No choice is 100% perfect, but some choices yield better benefits and that deserves your focus. It's also OK for your choices to change and evolve over time. Ultimately, it's all about how the choice impacts you and your family.

Margie also points out that children have an amazing ability to pull on your heart strings, which is why they can be masters of manipulation if you let them. She tells parents to refuse to play the game and give them the opportunity to grow more resourceful and resilient.

Recognise That Quality Is More Important Than Quantity

We can be with our kids 24/7 and yet never be fully present in the moment with them. Quality over quantity is most important. For me, it helps when my mobile phone is out of sight or I plan special trips to the restaurant, market or park. But ultimately, do what's best for you.

Don't Compare

What other mothers are doing is none of your business. Ultimately, what matters most is doing what works for you and your children to ensure that your family is happy and connected. It's time to lower the bar, get out of your own way, and enjoy the experience. Doing so won't hurt your children and it will free up precious energy so you can nurture your babies into well-rounded adults.

Avoid Social Media

Unfortunately, most of our FOMO insecurities stem from social media and being overly connected to everyone else's day-to-day lives. Michelle Minnikin, Chartered Business Psychologist and founder of Insights Business Psychology Ltd, confessed that it was only after she tracked her time on social media that she realised she had a problem. She was routinely spending 90 minutes a day on Facebook, Twitter, LinkedIn and Instagram. That's five hours per week, 45.5 hours per month and 13 weeks per year – just on social media. She notes: "If I could reduce that, I could spend more time with my family, or the equivalent of a whole week of work creating something useful that could generate income, or actually helping people, or volunteering my time. Anything but scrolling, liking, commenting."

Michelle believes that social media sites feed our FOMO. She recommends being more strategic and answering these questions for yourself: "Why am I using social media? How am I using this as a force for good? Is what I am sharing useful to others? What is the Return on Investment/Return on Energy?"

She also advises planning the week out on social media by scheduling content and spending an hour at the beginning of the week sharing content. Having regular 'office hours' for responding to questions from online groups and adding actual value could be helpful as it limits the time we spend on 'passive scrolling' when we are bored. She suggests doing something useful instead and focusing on enjoying your offline life. Reading a book, for example, can help reduce the negative impact of social media.

Embrace That You Are And Always Will Be Mummy

The emotional connection and influence you have over your child is incomparable. Your little cheeky monsters will always hold you close to their heart and consider you the most important person in their life well into adulthood.

Pause And Breathe

Never hesitate to press the pause button and breathe. Draw a line and know what's acceptable to forego and what's not. Give yourself permission to slow down and take a break from the lengthy to-do list. Don't you sometimes feel like that hamster running on the wheel? Ever since I became a mother, all my activities have been a mad swirl of rushed salon trips, rushed dinners and lunches, rushed work hours, rushed commute, rushed cooking, rushed parties as if there is a ticker in my mind. This type of break has more value than you might think – it provides a much-needed rest so you can pause the routine and collect yourself.

Working mum Victoria Beckham says that she loves getting on a plane and 'unplugging' because it is "the only time when [her] phone is switched off." She adds: "When you're a busy mum, you don't really have a lot of time to really, really relax. As a working mother, you should never feel guilty, you should feel proud. You're inspiring your children in the right way, being a strong woman going to work."

As a working mum who has had to miss many moments with her own son, I am well aware of the maternal sting that pierces the heart. There is also that irrational fear that your child might be closer to his care giver than he is to you, or that the care giver may know your child better than even you do. Guilt and exhaustion overwhelms you all the time. You are always in a quandary about the choices you make. You sometimes cry too. You are tired. But you are not a bad mum. You may be working out of necessity to provide for your children, or you may be working out of passion, but in doing so you are setting a great example for your children to follow their dreams.

In either case, you are not alone in treading this path.

Coping Strategies For FOMO

Accept That It's OK To Not Have It All At The Same Time

Install Home Cameras

Get Help

Appreciate The Value Of Playgroups And Daycare

Join Working Mum Networks

Know That Research Is In Your Favour

Use Empowering Language

Learn To Let Go

Don't Give In To Guilt

Recognise That Quality Is More Important Than Quantity

Don't Compare

Avoid Social Media

Embrace That You Are And Always Will Be Mummy

Pause And Breathe

CHAPTER 3:

IMPOSTOR SYNDROME

*It's not what you are that holds you back,
it's what you think you are not.*

Denis Waitley

Impostor Syndrome

45%

Let me begin by telling you a story. Seventeen years ago, a young girl chose to not show up at school to interview for the post of general secretary. She was too afraid and too shy. She dreaded the idea of sitting in a room across from seniors (albeit only two of them). Later, she was heartbroken by her lack of courage that caused her to miss out on an important opportunity. Luckily, opportunity knocked again. The society needed help and that's when she decided to *quietly* step up and start helping the teachers voluntarily. She did more than her fair share of work, had a terrific work ethic and was always on time. That commitment finally paid off! Her teacher advocates created a new position just for her – the post of vice president.

That day she learned something important: determination and consistency can win you results and earn you titles. She graduated with her picture in the school magazine. Apparently, her dream came true, right? Unfortunately, not quite! She earned her picture and her title, but what bothered her the most was that nobody knew her! Her friends who had bragged about their positions won important assignments outside school. But she didn't. That day she learned another important lesson. Sometimes consistency and determination are not enough. You need exposure too. Competence alone will not get you there. You will have to step up and show yourself; step up and ask; step up and showcase your contributions and achievements. But how could this girl do all this when she constantly felt insecure about her knowledge? Yes, she did well in class but that must be because of luck or the teacher being too kind!

Little did that girl know that what she was experiencing was the much dreaded Impostor Syndrome.

The 'Who Am I To Succeed?' Syndrome

We all feel inadequate at some point in our lives. Often it's when we don't recognise our own self-worth or believe we are qualified enough to achieve something. It's natural to feel 'not good enough' when we are pushed outside our comfort zone or trying something for the first time. Some people feel the same, despite being aware of their repeated, external evidence of competence. This fear or feeling is called Impostor Syndrome. Coined in 1978 by clinical psychologists Dr Pauline R Clance and Dr Suzanne A Imes, Impostor Syndrome is marked by a persistent fear of being exposed as a 'fraud' and an inability to internalise accomplishments.

I had these feelings when I trained senior managers. Every time I relocated to a different country and my target audience transitioned from local to global, I would feel inadequate – like I needed additional credentials to serve my new clients even though I already had international accreditations. If I only had one more qualification, one more training, I would be 'good enough' to do my job and be on a par with my colleagues.

I have often identified with these feelings but I didn't know what to label them. But they were always there, lurking in the back of my mind, even as I became more successful in my career. Many years later I was excited to discover these feelings had a name and they were, in fact, attributable to an actual syndrome. All the symptoms of this crippling syndrome were mine! This was me! And what's more, this disease cum syndrome apparently had a cure! I began to research and read more about it. And to my utter perverse sadistic delight, I discovered I wasn't the only one experiencing this disability. This bug had bitten lots of people!

Millions of people, including celebrities, athletes and CEOs have been plagued by constant self-doubt and feelings of unworthiness. Hollywood star Meryl Streep, Dr Chan, Chief of the World Health Organization, and Nobel Laureate Maya Angelou are all examples of famous people who have expressed inadequacy in their work, and hinted about the fear of being found out. Emma Watson, Sheryl Sandberg, Michelle Pfeiffer, Kate Winslet, Sonia Sotomayor and countless others have admitted to similar sentiments. High achievers, in particular, often doubt themselves and feel undeserving of the recognition they receive. While both men and women experience Impostor Syndrome, studies show that women are more often affected and thus likely to suffer the consequences. As Amy Cuddy says in her famous TED Talk: "I ended up at Princeton, and I was like, I am not supposed to be here. I am an impostor. I was so afraid of being found out."

In *The Confidence Code*, authors Katty Kan and Clare Shipman detail a meeting they had with Christine Lagarde who runs the International Monetary Fund. In their discussion, Christine reveals that she still worries about being caught off guard. "There are moments where I have to sort of go deep inside myself and pull my strength, confidence, background, history, experience and all the rest of it, to assert a particular point." The authors note they took a perverse sense of comfort from the fact that Christine shared their own feelings of inadequacies. I don't blame them. It's validating to know that you are not alone and it's perfectly normal to have such feelings, especially if this validation comes from powerful and high-profile women.

When I published my first article on Impostor Syndrome in the *HuffPost*, I received an overwhelming response. Lots of women in my circle started sending me texts and telling me how they could relate to the article. My blog was later re-published in *Thrive Global* and caught the attention of Arianna Huffington herself. She shared my blog on her Facebook, LinkedIn and Twitter feeds Within hours the blog shares and tweets amassed to more than 1,800 likes with hundreds of shares and retweets. As I became an overnight success, I realised the sheer intensity of this relatively unknown Impostor Syndrome! The more I wrote about it, the more traction it got and I started receiving invitations for talks on the syndrome. I was no expert and only a victim myself.

But hearing someone's first-hand experience is what many people needed to hear the most – that they are not alone and it's not just them. Years of training and my coaching and a Neuro Linguistic Programming certification allowed me to develop effective ways to overcome this syndrome using various coping strategies, and before I knew it, in the words of my client, I was "shepherding women away from the insidious Impostor Syndrome that permeates every stage of, specifically, women's careers."

Within my survey too, several women revealed that they have been plagued with Impostor Syndrome throughout their careers.

Alicia Engler, Vice President at Comsat who kindly volunteered to provide a detailed interview, noted in her interview that a male-dominated industry shaped how she saw herself. She shared how research has proven that when there are fewer than three women, they are neither heard nor validated, but three minutes later if a man says something similar, the same proposal is accepted without question.

Alicia was plagued by Impostor Syndrome throughout her career. While at college, she wished that she wasn't smart because she didn't know what to do to live up to that reputation. And I get that – having a reputation for something can be exhausting. Alicia says she was also impacted by FOMO up to a certain point, and she found it especially difficult to self-advocate and negotiate salaries until she learned how to do it effectively.

Jane Galloway, a director-level executive, reveals that as a self-diagnosed sufferer of Impostor Syndrome she can really relate to how it holds us back. When she saw herself described as a 'keynote speaker' in promotional materials for an upcoming event, her instinct was to think, well, those people are, but she shouldn't be up there. She confesses that it's a routine, internal struggle to avoid that type of damaging dialogue with herself. "Oh how I wish it was different!"

Dianne Greyson also identifies with Impostor Syndrome. She remembers being in a boardroom with a CEO, eight directors, and all of her nagging internal thoughts: What am I doing here? I shouldn't be here. But of course she should have been there!

Marie Sola, President at Daughters Of Change, shares this: "I would say that Impostor Syndrome is something that I had to learn to work through over the years, as I had no one to discuss this with when I was younger. When I started my own company, guess what tried to rear its ugly head? You've got it – Impostor Syndrome – that wicked, wicked monkey! Thankfully, I now have a great group of strong women who I can actually discuss it with and put that demon back in the corner where it belongs."

When I met Brianna, Impostor Syndrome was one of the first things we discussed. In Brianna's words: "It keeps coming back up in so many different forms, eg I've written x, y and z, but I couldn't possibly call myself 'a writer'. Or, I don't have enough experience for that post so I won't apply, and I've definitely seen a lot of deflection of responsibility for achievements, which of course is feeding all of this. I find it especially upsetting as this plays a role in our contributions in life – in the workplace, but also in casual personal conversations! Feeling like we need to qualify opinions or experiences, rather than owning them. I've read books on feminism by female authors with large qualifying paragraphs as to why they have an opinion on the subject and thus have the ability to speak on it. And I think this plays a big role in the analysis paralysis that I, and many women I know, experience. We refuse to confidently take action or put something out there until the decision or product has been picked apart and approached from every angle to ensure we deserve to take up that space (rather than be branded an impostor!). It's scary thinking about all the untapped or halted potential due to this occurrence, and how it intersects with other challenges like being young for your field, or a woman, or returning to work, or caring for children."

I couldn't agree more. Even though I teach strategies to overcome Impostor Syndrome, I often experience it myself from time to time. For example, just before sharing my survey analysis on LinkedIn, I went through an analysis paralysis of whether the information was comprehensive or worthy enough. I spent a great deal of time editing the text and main idea to make it appear as objective as it could be. Then I thought about the main purpose of this post, which was to let women know that they are not alone in their challenges, and that there are many who face similar issues (as the survey results supported). That's when I finally stopped overanalysing it.

For a long time I thought I should colour my hair white or wear it in a bun, wear higher heels and specs to look older and more experienced, especially when I was training people twice my age. Those types of limiting beliefs can really thwart your self-image and progress. Thinking about purpose rather than 'perfection' has helped me overcome this issue. Brianna, too, confessed to buying glasses in her early twenties (glasses she didn't need) for exactly the same reasons I did!

Another ghostwriter friend revealed that a number of people experience self-doubt when it comes to writing their first book. They wonder if there's a point to their book and if it will truly help others. These people are experts in their fields with 20+ years of experience, and yet even with their degrees they feel like impostors.

Laurie said: "I doubt myself (my talents/instincts/knowledge) regularly. I'm not as much of a perfectionist as I used to be, thank goodness, but it's still there occasionally." Kelsey Lindsay also says that Impostor Syndrome is her leading challenge. "I'm starting a new job (same field, different company) in a couple of weeks and I'm so anxious."

Susie Barry says this syndrome has plagued her entire life and Colleen shares that it kept her from advancing: "I felt I didn't have what it took to be a doctor. I feel the same way about parenting. I feel I'm only passable. My main problem may be I just don't ever reach my own ideal, and maybe I always keep that just out of reach."

Yoko Lytle is another victim of Impostor Syndrome. "[I feel] a lack of motivation to actually be better at my job... cause I have that 'what's the point?' voice in my head. If I don't try I can't fail, right?!'"

For women who venture to start their own business, the self-doubt issues creep in there too. Over a three-month period from September to December 2017, enterprise consultant Daniella Genas conducted research with 162 women to understand the challenges, barriers and motivations they faced starting and/or growing a business. Daniella very kindly shared her research with me when I was researching for my book. According to both interviews and questionnaires, lack of confidence was a prevalent theme with respondents across all business stages:

"Some respondents had long and successful industry careers but still believed that this was not enough to be successful in business. Several participants expressed that they had purposely delayed trying to scale their business and/or missed out on pursuing opportunities because they did not believe they would be successful. Additionally, many growth stage respondents were uncomfortable being called female entrepreneurs as they considered the term 'entrepreneur' more appropriate for someone like Richard Branson. This was regardless of the fact that these women actually fitted the definition of entrepreneur. A few respondents expressed fear that they would one day be 'found out' for not being as amazing or inspirational as people kept saying they were. Others believed they required business specific training before they felt ready to truly start a business."

This extensive research proves that women face self-doubt issues not just as career women but business owners too.

In the first chapter, I highlighted the many different ways women have faced more discrimination and judgment than their male counterparts have. Society has conditioned us to develop all these internal challenges, and Impostor Syndrome is no different. Perhaps, it's also the leading example of what conditioning and cultural implications can do to you.

Valerie Young, author of *The Secret Thoughts of Successful Women*, says: "Being female means you and your work automatically stand a greater chance of being ignored, discounted, trivialised, devalued or otherwise taken less seriously than a man's." It is therefore no surprise that women tend to question their abilities and feel inferior, all the more because traditionally and culturally that's what they have been accustomed to for their entire life. Women in positions of power are given much less latitude than their male peers in terms of appearance, behaviour, judgment, the tenor of their voice… everything.

According to Valerie you are most impacted by Impostor Syndrome if: you work within the creative field; you are a stranger in a strange land; you are a student; you work in an organisation culture that feeds self-doubt; or if you represent your entire social group. Dr Pauline Clance and Dr Suzanne Imes, and various other collaborators, highlight four coping mechanisms to manage impostor feelings: diligence and hard work, holding back, use of charm, and procrastination. Valerie adds three more to the list: maintaining a low or ever-changing profile, never finishing, and self-sabotage.

During my survey, I discovered some very interesting findings which substantiated the research I did. Professor of Education at Harvard and a pioneer in studying the development of girls, Dr Carol Gilligan's research for the American Association reveals an interesting data point: girls losing confidence is not attributed to hormones. As she notes: "If that was it, then the loss of self-esteem would happen to all girls and at roughly the same time." But that wasn't the case. In fact what was fascinating was that black women turned out to be more confident than their white female counterparts.

Glamour teamed up with L'Oréal Paris to conduct a survey of 2,000 women in all 50 states. The survey takes an in-depth look at factors that buoy and undermine our confidence. In survey question after survey question, a pattern emerged: black women consistently reported higher self-esteem than white or Hispanic women, and – among other things – they were far more likely to describe themselves as successful. Black women consider themselves successful and beautiful, and have a much higher level of body positivity. These results may seem odd, since black women are routine victims of systemic racism and sexism.

In reference to this survey, Marquaysa Battle writes: "As a black woman, this surprises me very little. I was raised, like a lot of other black women that I know, to have confidence and to give myself credit in areas that racism and discrimination might lead the world to never give me. We were taught in the home that the one thing we would certainly have to learn to do was to acknowledge and celebrate ourselves, while expecting little from mainstream (read: white) America."

The American Association researchers confirmed the same. They concluded that black girls drew their apparent self-confidence from their families and communities rather than from the school system. Study advisor Janie Victoria Ward, a Rockefeller fellow at the University of Pennsylvania who is studying the socialisation of black families, said one factor that might help black girls is that they are often surrounded by strong women they admire. Black women are more likely than others to have a full-time job and run a household. Another factor, she said, may be that black parents often teach their children there is nothing wrong with them, only with the way the world treats them.

My own survey yielded similar results for Asian women. Comparatively, fewer Asian women faced self-confidence and Impostor Syndrome issues. Their challenges were more to do with misogynist work environments, FOMO and even getting permission to work!

This got me thinking. What are these Asian women doing differently? Why aren't they as consumed with self-doubt as American and European women? I realised what it was: these Asian career women have to be confident and own their role out of necessity given their fundamental challenge is so basic – earning the right to work. To fight the external challenges, they first master their internal challenges.

That said, Asian and black women who were also expats and immigrants working outside familiar territories do tend to experience a higher degree of Impostor Syndrome. As Jazimine Gomez states in her article *How These Latinos Got Over Impostor Syndrome*: "For people of colour, Impostor Syndrome comes in a racialised way." A University of Texas at Austin study of 322 'ethnic minority college students' found that students were aware of the stereotypes associated with their racial/ethnic groups, and that influenced how they experienced the syndrome.

The Feelings Around Impostor Syndrome

As Valerie Young pointed out, you would have to have achieved something in life to feel fraudulent about – something which you hadn't anticipated or mastered, or not at least according to your ridiculously high standards.

When you start facing insecurities related to your knowledge base or skillset, when you start explaining successes, chalking the latter to luck, or when you find yourself minimising evidence of your success, that's when you know you have been touched by the impostor wand. Some of the common feelings associated with this syndrome include the following:

'I must not fail.'

'I feel like a fake.'

'It's all down to luck.'

'I don't deserve this.'

'Someone must have made a mistake.'

'Success is no big deal.'

'What if they find out that I am not as smart as they think?'

'Can I really pull this off?'

'Who do I think I am?'

'I got lucky.'

'I was in the right place at the right time.'

'If I can do it, so can you.'

'I had help.'

'They made a terrible mistake.'

'I had connections.'

'They are just being nice.'

'They felt sorry for me.'

'I have fooled others.'

Is Impostor Syndrome Always A Bad Thing?

Let me clarify an important point: Impostor Syndrome is not always bad and it's not necessarily a confidence issue. If it was, then many high-achieving women wouldn't be successful at all. Impostor Syndrome is having an incorrect assessment of your worthiness and successes, and that in turn may impact your confidence depending on the degree to which you undermine your own talent. If your self-doubt isn't impeding your progress, but rather encouraging you to work harder towards mastering or perfecting a skill, it's healthy self-doubt. Many people think that confidence is overrated, they may be right! Sometimes, self-doubt can be more positive than negative. I have talked to many amazing women regarding Impostor Syndrome and we discussed how a healthy dose of it might benefit some people we know! 'Male Answer Syndrome' 'Irrational Self Syndrome' are real life syndromes affecting many people!

The whole problem with the world is that fools and
fanatics are always so certain of themselves,
and wiser people so full of doubts.

Bertrand Russell

To me confidence entails knowing when to step up and make yourself heard, but also knowing when to back down and prepare some more to maximise your contributions. There is a fine line between confidence and overconfidence.

However, when low self-esteem and that feeling of being a fraud or impostor stops you from stepping up, or it starts taking a toll on your health, then that's when you need to develop coping mechanisms.

A few months back I 'dared' to raise my hand to answer a question asked at a working lunch. The question was: "How many of you think that you have a strong personal brand?" I promptly raised my hand – I was surprised at my own audacity. A few years back I would never have dreamed of raising my hand. But at that moment I knew I had a reason to raise my hand. Ever since I began living as an expat, I have made conscious and consistent efforts to promote myself and build my own personal brand. I may not be 'world-famous' in this market but I have made a name for myself. The impostor in me has pushed me to work hard, so in this case it has been a positive force for personal development.

Candyce Costa shares her experience with Impostor Syndrome and how she piled on her certifications to prove her self-worth. In my discussion with her, she highlights how Impostor Syndrome has both helped her and held her back. She writes:

> *"I've decided to work as a freelancer after quitting my job. My first thought was: you are not good enough, people cannot trust you because you have no knowledge. And I fight back: of course I am good. I am no guru but good enough. To hear back: are you? In 15 months I've done 10 different certified courses and many more: digital marketing, social media management, social media and reputation, started a Business and Marketing diploma, done Google and WordPress, many different crash courses in marketing from Hootsuite, HubSpot and so many webinars and online courses from gurus. I've learned a lot, don't get me wrong, but every time, every additional certification only served to further validate my knowledge, reaffirm my confidence and make me feel good.*

I placed immense pressure on myself but the positives are there: had it not been for the Impostor Syndrome probably I would not have dedicated so much time, effort and money studying and upgrading my knowledge. Maybe I would not have done so much and prove to myself that I am good enough. I think I've just developed a love/hate relationship with my Impostor Syndrome voice."

Money mind expert Gull Khan also views Impostor Syndrome as a positive force: "Impostor Syndrome was my biggest hurdle in the past. Even after receiving great academic results from my A levels to BVC exams, passing NY Bar exams (which are notoriously hard), I still felt inadequate. Then when I changed careers again I suffered from this Impostor Syndrome even though I achieved great success. But I have come to terms with this Impostor Syndrome. I now use it positively to make sure I am forever bettering myself, so becoming even greater at my craft, to endeavour to help my clients get even better and faster results. I use it to stop becoming complacent and use it as a motivational force."

Sometimes, the impostor in us makes us realise that we can't continue running on the wheel in the exact same way – it won't work. Most impostors know that it's important to change their old way of doing things if they want to earn new assignments or projects. In such situations, appearing brash and overconfident can often work to our own detriment. No matter how good you are, chances are there are still things that you don't know. Accepting that sooner rather than later can be the first step towards managing a challenging situation. Whether you are an entrepreneur or working professional, Impostor Syndrome can give us the drive to continuously learn more and reinvent ourselves.

As noted, confidence is not just a mindset or attitude, it's also knowing the right time to step up or stay down. Yes, a little extra confidence helps in good measure in the face of uncertainty. However, there is no denying that confidence that emanates from mastery and expertise is authentic. And we don't always have to speak first or dominate the conversation. We can choose to listen. Sometimes confidence can be quiet!

Stepping up without knowledge, preparation or practice might be perceived as vanity, and if the impostor in you is saying 'don't do it' then listen to your internal voice. If you know what you are talking about and have prepared adequately, yet the impostor in you still pushes you to stay silent, then that is a voice to ignore. Punch it in its theoretical face, then get up and do it anyway – ***own it!*** Just like I owned it at that lunch. In truth, there are many days when self-doubt overwhelms me despite my own coping strategies. But not on that day. On that day and at that particular moment, I knew I had conquered the 'impostor' in me. It was a great feeling.

Coping Strategies For Impostor Syndrome

Be Aware Of Your Feelings

The first step is to recognise your feelings. Self-awareness is the key to effecting change in the way you think and act. The moment you recognise your feelings, you are opening yourself up to different strategies to manage it.

Humans are complex, and at any given time you can be occupied with an influx of emotions, concerns and problems bouncing up and down in your head all at once. That's why it's a good idea to document your feelings by penning them down.

Committing everything to paper can also be compared to performing a brain dump or 'letting it all out'. This lets you clearly sift through muddy, confused thoughts to expose your raw emotions and pinpoint the exact emotion or feeling.

In separating emotion from rational thought, it then becomes easier to let your intellect dictate your choices and get some clarity around your experiences. After all, your thoughts are your inner dialogue. Very simply, you want to become aware of what you tell yourself inside so that you – rather than your emotions – direct your choices.

Make a list of triggers for your self-doubt. Select one trigger at a time. Pause for a moment to take three to five slow, deep breaths from the belly, and allow yourself to relax. Keep your eyes closed and focus on your breath. Scan your entire body from the top of your head to the tips of your toes, finding and releasing any tension or tightness. Take note of any sensations. Accept and acknowledge the feelings.

Imagine yourself in a safe place and find your centre. Remind yourself you are not your emotions or thoughts. You observe, create and choose your emotions and thoughts. No one and no situation can 'make' you feel a certain way without your permission. Understand that any emotions you experience are merely old pockets of energy – social conditioning – from a time when you did not have the cognitive ability to know and see yourself and your life from many different perspectives. Now, as an intelligent, capable adult, you are fully in charge of your feelings.

Find Other 'Infected' People

There are many others who share the same fears as you. By sharing your concerns you will likely discover that you are not in this alone, which makes the fear more tolerable. Seek support from those who identify with your issues and have effectively conquered them. You might even benefit from joining a support or affinity group.

Reframe The Context Of The Situation By Self-Questioning Limiting Beliefs

Remember when you wanted to pursue a goal but didn't because you failed the first time? Or the time when you didn't voice your opinion in a meeting for fear of being rejected or judged? In both cases those are limiting beliefs holding you back. A limiting belief is a false belief that a person holds true based on incorrect or incomplete conclusions about certain things in life. Impostor Syndrome is one such negative belief.

Human beings have a tendency to be negative and some are more prone to it than others. However, when these beliefs turn into toxic thought traps that sabotage your own progress, they need to be addressed promptly. The good news is that with a little practice and discipline, you can avoid succumbing to these naughty mind-chattering gremlins and stop them right in their tracks.

In difficult situations, people often find themselves unable to think clearly, so they seek out advice from others. But unless you consult a qualified coach who can help you manage the problem effectively, most others will likely make the situation worse by passing on their own negativity to you. Hence, other than a coach, it is always best to rely on yourself. An effective way to do this is through self-questioning. Self-questioning involves scrutinising your beliefs and examining the actions you take as a result of them.

There are many different types of limiting beliefs, including: generalisations, mental filters, emotional reasoning, distortions, magnifications, labelling, etc. You can subvert each one by testing its validity through a belief-audit that enables you to identify holes in your thinking. The moment you encounter a limiting belief, you can question it using the four different techniques listed below.

Question Its Generality

Find out if the belief is based on any general/one-size fits all type of conclusion. Ask yourself if the belief always hold true or if this is a one-off instance. Has there ever been a time when you felt confident or different from how you do now? If yes, what were those circumstances? This will help you differentiate situations where the belief did not hold true from the times when it did, thereby making you realise that the situation is not always as black or white, 'all or nothing' as you think. This understanding, in turn, restores feelings of hope and trust and rebuilds your confidence. It also helps you acknowledge positive elements of a situation, creates positive vibes, and helps regain and maintain control.

Question Its Authenticity

Evaluate the subjectivity of the belief by ascertaining if it's based on limited or incomplete knowledge and/or opinions versus facts. If it's based on opinions, evaluate whether you can trust the source of that opinion. Substantiate the belief with evidence that can support or negate it, while considering all factors surrounding the belief including any previously ignored influences. Often our suppositions are only partially true and thus lack factual evidence. Once you learn to identify unverified beliefs, you will become open to more enabling points of view which could be equally true. Remember, the Earth was considered flat until proved otherwise.

If the belief leads you to a decision, then assess if it's leading you to accept responsibility whether or not this was in your control. Alternatively, take into account instances where you fail to own up to your mistake. And finally, think about what someone you trust would say about your conclusion.

Question Its Context

Some negative beliefs emerge as a result of various factors and influences – the absence or presence of which can lead to a change in that belief. Ask yourself if your speculation is owing to the context of the situation or a specific phase. These phases often involve our relationships with people and could include triggers such as a crucial period at work, a new job, a new responsibility or role, a transition period, a relocation etc. This will allow you to see your belief in relation to various factors impacting it and thus give it a wider perspective as opposed to viewing it in isolation.

If the belief involves people, examine scenarios that could be involved in affecting thoughts and actions – for example: loneliness, depression, boredom, old age, insecurity, fears of losing or missing out, or health issues. Identifying triggers provides fresh perspective on a situation; most people react differently to different situations. You cannot expect a calm, poised response from an otherwise composed person if he/she is enduring a challenging life event.

If a relationship has been stuck in a specific phase, could it be that the person involved is reacting the only way he/she knows how and is unaware of a better way to react?

Also, do not disregard timing to be a factor responsible for shaping your belief in a certain way. Ask yourself: will this belief be different a few weeks from now when the timing is more favourable?

It becomes easier to understand why we may have negative surmises regarding situations or people when we begin to identify and connect with the context and understand the real reasons driving people as well as our own behaviour. Try replacing the negative opinions with more enabling beliefs by reframing them in a positive light.

You can also ask yourself if there is anything you can do or should have done to improve the situation for this person. Empathy coupled with practical solutions can go a long way. Think of ways you can help. Have you exhausted all efforts or are there still a few things left you can try? This analysis will move you off a self-pitying or resentful path and on to one that is more constructive and solution-oriented.

NLP (Neuro Linguistic Programming) also helps you in understanding the 'context' of any situation better. I decided to pursue formal NLP qualification two years ago. This certification adds credibility to my training and HR consultancy practice, but I had personal reasons for joining the class too. Four years ago I lost my father to a sudden heart attack. Ever since, I had been overwhelmed by a strong sense of unresolved grief – a condition I thought NLP might help me with. Others had rave reviews about the positive changes they realised after completing the class so I was eager to learn more about it. That said, I was also quite sceptical that it would have a major impact on me.

After just the first day of training, I instantly realised why people claimed it transformed their lives! There are many fantastic NLP presuppositions that are the foundation of Neuro Linguistic Programming. I will only be sharing those that can help you understand the context of any situation in a better light. The following two strategies will also help you in Chapter 9 when you are learning how to lead in male-dominated industries.

The first is that ***everyone has a unique map of the world and each one responds to it differently.*** Our responses and actions are moulded by our own perceptions and personal experiences. What one party deems appropriate might seem unreasonable to others. And that's because their judgments are informed by their own personal views versus ours. This powerful concept explains why some people react so differently from each other in similar situations.

Do you often feel frustrated with someone for what he/she does or does not do? (Hint: think of some men at your workplace.) Well that's because, simply put, ***he is not you***! His perceptions, perspectives and model of the world inform how he acts and reacts, and his map is different from yours. What's more, his social conditioning is dramatically different from yours too. Think of any objection, concern or complaint you have had with someone in the recent past: *Why is she so aggressive? Why is he so submissive? Why can't she stand up for herself? Why doesn't she reciprocate love and kindness the same way I do? Why is he always so negative? Why is she so cold and expressionless? Why can't she move on and get over it? What? She has already moved on? But why?*

These and many more similar questions will often arise as you interact with people in your everyday life and particularly at work. It is natural to be affected by the choices people you are surrounded with make. However, when you start acknowledging 'the difference in maps' across various individuals in your life, you can better understand why they react the way they do. I am not suggesting that NLP will help you transcend to an extraordinary, ethereal level of total positivity, but with this new understanding, you may already be looking at different situations and people with a more empathetic light in your eyes!

The second NLP presupposition which helped me understand the context of any situation is that ***the meaning of communication is the response you get.*** Communication style also plays an important role in how you handle a situation. Many times, people come across as negative only because they fail to express themselves appropriately. At work or even at home we often feel exasperated for not being understood. *Why doesn't she listen? Why is it so difficult for him to understand?* This is where the NLP assumption comes in handy! In every communication, our purpose is to influence the receiver. It could be through an emotion, advice, instruction, statement or a combination of all of these. This communication will only have purpose and meaning if the recipient responds in the way you intended.

I once had an assistant who habitually misunderstood every instruction I gave her. It annoyed me profusely. NLP helped me realise that my communication failure with her was more my fault than hers! You see, before asking her to do anything I had already made up my mind that this instruction would *have* to be reiterated several times before I could expect it to be executed smoothly. As a result, my requests were couched in vague details and delivered via a frustrated tone of voice she could certainly detect. If I had worked to improve both the method and delivery of my requests until I received the desired response, then I would have saved both of us a great deal of time and energy.

Communication variations include adjusting the tone and volume of your voice, employing facial expressions, making eye contact, and choosing and articulating your words thoughtfully. Ask yourself the following questions: Are you using jargon? Have you given too many instructions at once? Did you omit important details? Is your tone too gentle or too firm? Are you squinting your eyes or furrowing your brows? Are you making eye contact? Is the eye contact too intimidating? Do you look interested or bored or tired?

The best way to know if you are on the same page as the recipient is to gauge his reactions and response; if they seem satisfactory then continue; if not then consider the previous questions and reassess your communication style. To summarise, any communication you initiate carries with it the responsibility of delivering a positive impact. Once you believe in this concept and start truly owning your personal communication, you will be an even better communicator than you already are.

These two foundational NLP principles really helped me re-evaluate my relationships with several people, including work relationships. It also changed the way I perceived them. To be honest, it was quite liberating. After all, harbouring grievances and holding on to grudges can be quite draining. It's OK to feel resentful on occasion, but when it permeates your every thought and saps your energy, remind yourself that his map is different from yours and move on.

Question Its Impact

Evaluate the impact of what could go wrong by asking yourself what could be the worst consequence of holding this belief and how will it affect you. This will help mitigate your fear. They say anything that doesn't kill you only makes you stronger. In most cases, what you anticipate as the worst outcome is never as frightening as you thought it would be. When you realise this, you will feel more prepared to face whatever consequences arise from it. Ask yourself: What would I do if I were being more courageous? What will inaction/doing nothing cost me one year from now? Is my fear of failure causing me to overestimate risk, and holding myself back from taking risks that would serve me (my career/ business etc)?

Negative thinking can be an energy vampire that severely limits your ability to achieve your objectives. These questioning tactics can distance you from debilitating thoughts and allow you to view situations more objectively. However, for self-questioning to be most effective, you must stop believing in the myth that someone else will come to your rescue. Trust yourself to be your own best rescuer, simply because who else could be a better expert in your life than *you* yourself? Ultimately, you own and control the most powerful weapon that can help you to get out of your own way – your brain. Do not underestimate its power; it will play a pivotal role in making any of your efforts successful and empower you to make well-informed decisions regarding any situation or relationship, free from personal biases and subjectivity.

By repeatedly telling your brain that it can achieve something, you can train it to think affirmatively. Make sure you feed it with only positive and 'can do' thoughts. As Henry Ford aptly put it: "Whether you think you can, or you think you can't, you're probably right."

Helpful Questions To Overcome Limiting Beliefs

Is this belief always true?

Am I making any assumptions?

Is my belief based on limited and incomplete knowledge?

What proof/evidence is there to support my belief or negate it?

What other factors do I need to consider?

What would someone I trust think of my conclusion?

Who says things should be this way?

How else might I view this situation?

Am I accepting responsibility for something which is not my fault or within my control?

What am I not seeing or acknowledging?

What could be a more enabling belief?

What's the worst that can happen?

What is the Opportunity Cost of Inaction?

Work On Self-Belief By Rewiring Your Brain For Success

Remember the girl we talked about in the beginning of the chapter. She was the shy type who struggled to string sentences together. Yes, that girl. She soon realised what she needed: an attribute that could help her achieve what she hadn't so far. With that realisation, as if by magic, there was no looking back.

It was this very attribute which, only a year later, helped her ace her public speaking class, become founder and president of the first HR society at her college, and address a room of hundreds with ease and confidence. This one attribute helped her network with senior professionals and get her point across successfully. It also helped her get her first job at the age of 22 when all her other classmates were still studying. This one valuable attribute ensured she was the youngest manager at work, training people twice her age and level. This one attribute landed her consecutive promotions and multiple job offers across every interview she took. This one attribute helped her launch not one, but several, of her own companies in different parts of the world.

Seventeen years, three companies and three countries ago that girl hadn't showed up for the History Society interview. And yet today, nothing gives her more of an adrenaline rush than speaking to a room full of people. She has now trained thousands from various nationalities and ethnicities in 38 different soft skills. Not long ago she even trained a room full of high-profile police officials! Again, all due to that one attribute! That young girl is now a wife, mother, entrepreneur, and owner of three different brands. Want to know who she is? Well, that young girl's story is **my** story, and the one attribute that transformed my life considerably is **self-belief**: *if you think you can, then you will.*

Confidence is really a state of mind. A conscious choice. A deliberate decision. Your success depends on the state of your mind and you can transform this state of mind as well as positively impact it by working on your self-belief. Self-belief is the understanding that you can do what you set out to do. I have often emphasised in my articles, training and podcasts, and in the earlier strategy, how crucial it is to send positive signals to your brain and make it believe that it can achieve something even when the situation is not favourable.

No one except you should make life decisions on your behalf, and moreover, no one should have the power to disengage you and negatively influence you. You can't control what people around you will think and say, but you can control your own reaction and avoid the taint of negativity.

Believing in myself changed my life in unimaginable ways. But self-belief doesn't come easily. It requires practice and conviction and a careful rewiring of your brain. To believe in yourself, you first need to convince your brain that it can and will achieve what you want it to do. You see, the brain will do exactly as it's told. If you keep telling yourself that you can do something, you will be amazed by how well your brain cooperates in reaching that goal. And that's why repeatedly feeding your brain with positive affirmations is the first step towards success.

In this section, I am going to share the exact techniques that helped me train my brain for success. I'm betting they can also help you.

The first helpful strategy is to *Express Your Goals Using Positive and Empowering Language.*

One powerful way to rewire your brain towards achievement is to use 'towards-based motivation'. State your outcome in terms of positively expressed goals versus avoidance goals. Choose the words and then write them down in a positive frame. *Language can affect results.* Simply start by expressing what you *do want* instead of what you *don't want.* Effectively, you edit the word 'don't' out of your vocabulary. Focus on what you want to happen and not what you want to avoid, because ultimately, what you focus on is what you get more of.

"If you haven't got what you want, it's because you're not communicating correctly with your mind," says psychologist, best-selling author and motivational speaker Marisa Peer. She further adds that "the brain does what it thinks you want so you have to be very careful when telling your brain what you want."

Marisa also encourages talking yourself out of negativity and challenging situations by using empowering language such as: 'I want to do it; I choose to do it; I love doing it'. By replacing disempowering phrases like 'I have to' with empowering ones like 'I choose to', you are removing yourself from a victim position and putting yourself in control. You will feel fully in charge of your actions and that will eventually impact how you approach challenging situations in the future.

The next important way in which you can rewire your brain *is to Tell It Exactly What You Want by Visualising the Outcome Using Sensory Words.*

Tell your mind what you want by using detailed, precise, descriptive and powerful words. In a blog titled *How to Arouse the Magic of Sensory Words*, the author Henneke says: "Sensory words are more powerful and memorable than ordinary words because they make your reader see, hear, smell, taste, or feel your words. When reading non-sensory words, your brain processes text. But when you read sensory words, different areas of your brain light up. Your brain processes sensory words as if you taste a sweet cake, as if you see a dazzling display of colours, or as if you feel a rough texture."

Imagining the outcome is your biggest secret to success. Visualisation involves using your imagination and actively thinking what you'd really like to accomplish. Athletes and personal coaches are big supporters of visualisation techniques because they are so effective. Athletes often visualise the vivid and colourful image of wearing a gold medal on the podium or hoisting the World Cup. Visualising what you want builds emotional engagement and inspiration behind the goal.

Determine it in your mind. ***Think of the goal as if it were already yours*** and what you and/or the things around you will look/sound/ feel like when you achieve the goal. Focus on how good that feels and what the benefit is to you by using as many sensory-based words as you can. When you imagine the outcome with all senses involved – what you would see, hear, feel when it is being achieved – the goal becomes compelling and the ownership increases. Remember, whatever you tell your mind, it will believe, so be sure to tell it great things.

The third effective step for rewiring your brain is *Linking Massive Pleasure with Achieving a Goal and Pain with Lack of Achievement/ Maintaining the Status Quo*.

Everything we do in our life is driven by the twin forces of pain and pleasure. Commonly referred to as punishment and reward, they drive us to seek to avoid pain or gain pleasure. The key to creating a change is to associate our action/goal with massive pain when we don't do it and massive pleasure when we do. By linking pain and pleasure to our goals, we propel ourselves in the direction of our goals. All success is a result of attaching massive pain and massive pleasure to our goals. The more we link pleasure and pain to our outcomes, the greater is our desire to reach our outcomes. Pleasure and pain are also basic and intrinsic principles of human behaviour. Make a note of the price you would pay for protection and opportunities you would miss. Similarly, focus on the benefits and exhilaration you will experience as a result of achieving a goal. Personally, this technique always does wonders for me.

These three techniques will help bring you closer to your goals and outcomes as you rewire your brain for success. Of course, these alone are not enough. Hard work, determination and knowledge also play a role. As I wrote in my *HuffPost* article on *Limiting Beliefs*: "You need to stop believing in the myth that someone else will come to your rescue; believe in yourself instead."

Use The Brain Flip

I recently conducted a webinar with my friend and confidence coach, Elsewine, about Stepping up Your Stage Confidence. Given the positive feedback I received, I'd like to share one technique from that material which helps me manage any stage jitters. It's called

The Brain Flip. The minute I find myself encountering a negative thought, I count to three and immediately flip it, or replace it, with a positive thought. For example, a thought like 'There are such amazing people on stage today, who am I to be here?' 3…2…1 **insert the flip:** 'I *love* speaking on stage! The moment I hold the mic, I get such an adrenaline rush that I will start speaking energetically and confidently so much so that everyone will notice and acknowledge me!'

You see? The brain feeds on your thought process and acts accordingly. I know that if I allow my negative thoughts to linger for too long, they will gradually overtake me and permeate every cell of my body to the extent that when I walk on stage, I will be shaky and unsure. However, Brain Flip ensures that I flush out any toxic thoughts and only focus on the positive ones, so when I confront hundreds of people, every ounce of my existence is reflecting that positivity back.

Reaffirm Your Self-Worth And Own Your Success

Despite being confident, women are still reluctant to step forward, compete for lead roles and take risks. When girls are complimented for their achievements, they also tend to deflect praise and keep their accomplishments low key. By laying low they feel they are shielding themselves from scrutiny. There was a time when I stopped sharing my achievements for fear of being labelled as boastful. Thankfully, my mentor coached me out of that. *Lean In* shares that some girls don't speak up in class unless they're 100% sure they have the right answer, while others shy away from trying new subjects or activities.

This same reluctance also holds women back. Don't shy away or dismiss compliments by attributing your success to external factors. Accept your success and be kind to yourself. Own it! When you feel undeserving, go back and review previous accomplishments or positive feedback. Recount the people you made a difference for.

This will help assure you that nobody belongs here more than you do. No one is telling you to be ostentatious, but downplaying your success will help no one.

Last year I went to watch *Cars 3* with three excited boys – my two nephews and my son. My son had been eagerly anticipating the film for many months, so even though I was not an avid fan of the series, I knew I had to take him as soon as it came out because he knew the release date and was counting down the days (isn't it fascinating that six-year-olds know their favourite film's release date even before you do?). Most children's films awaken the child within me, but admittedly, some can be quite boring; I have even dozed off while watching a few (ssh… don't tell my son). Honestly, I thought *Cars 3* would be one of those. But to my surprise, it turned out to be exactly the opposite! I watched the film with the same nail-biting enthusiasm as the boys. *Cars 3* is by far one of the most inspirational films I have seen in the past few months, possibly even years.

As I sat there nibbling popcorn and Maltesers, I was mentally taking notes of all the great lines from the film. I had to share them not only to remind my son, but also reinforce the wonderful lessons they offered to me and those I coach. To my surprise, when I searched online for the exact quotes, I discovered many articles discussing the valuable leadership lessons within the film. The movie reinforces some important lessons on self-confidence and managing adversity, The Lightning McQueen way!

Cars 3 demonstrates that impostor feelings are very real, but with the right support, they can be overcome. In the film, Cruz Ramirez's story is a classic example of someone suffering from Impostor Syndrome. She was unsure of herself and so her self-doubt prevented her from following her dreams and putting herself forward.

In her blog entitled *Cars 3's Cruz Ramirez Knows All About Impostor Syndrome*, author Amy Ratcliffe writes: "Cruz is every person who's ever experienced the unnerving tendrils of Impostor Syndrome wrapping around their brain. Cruz is every person who's ever experienced a lack of confidence. For many of us, particularly for many women I know, Cruz is the very picture of relatable. Though it's not strictly a gender issue, the confidence gap does exist. In many situations, especially in the workforce, women are less self-assured than men."

Even though Cruz did not believe she could win the race, she was able to let go of her fears and outperform her competitors after receiving the right motivation and encouragement. This is one of my favourite exchanges in the film:

Jackson Storm: You don't belong on this track.

Cruz: Yesss I do!!!!

This last statement teaches you about owning your success and believing in yourself. The moment you believe that you belong where you are and deserve to be there, you will start flying! Watch out for those newfound wings!

Women tend to externalise success by attributing it to factors. Impostor Syndrome expert, Valerie Young, recommends the following exercise. Create a list of your achievements and determine what role luck, timing and connections played in realising your success. Write down the specific actions you took to get somewhere. Documenting your successes and the exact steps you took to get there will help you realise that what you achieved wasn't just luck. You may have been in the right place at the right time, but opportunity favours those who are most prepared.

Earlier this year, I was nominated for two prestigious awards. The night I found out I couldn't sleep at all. I was happy but restless. It was like I couldn't own my success. I kept asking myself 'Why me?' I had only moved to London two years earlier. Surely there were more deserving people. What have I done? The next morning my husband sat me down and asked me very solemnly:

"Hira, have you bribed your way into it?"

"Of course not," I replied indignantly.

"Well, you must have done something to be nominated. Someone must have thought you are worthy and that's why you were nominated in the first place. Can you recall?" he replied.

I began to list whatever I had done in the past two years. In my own mind, there was a lot left to be done and I had merely scratched the surface of what I wanted to accomplish. However, what I considered to be little accomplishments were actually quite large by many standards. And do you know what? I slept peacefully that night.

Sometimes, we need these reality checks to realise our own worth. It may not be much according to your own self-imposed, lofty goals, but somewhere, someone thinks you have done a great job. Don't deny or belittle that. Don't start looking for excuses to justify that success. Acknowledge it gracefully. Own it. Say thank you.

Remind yourself that you achieved what you did because you did something different – something extra, something you believed in, something that others didn't do or try. The world needs believers, innovators and doers, someone they can look up to, someone who can inspire them to try even when they are unsure.

Practise Confidence By Deploying Certain Strategies

Report after report indicates that women are inching their way into senior leadership positions at a snail's pace even though they are already very hard-working, possess strong work ethics and are regularly outpacing men in all disciplines with university degrees. So what else is holding them back? The co-founders of *Breakthrough: For Women Leaders on the Fast Track*, note: "Confidence is the underlying issue permeating all of leadership presence."

You don't necessarily need to be confident from inside; it's more important to look confident from the outside. Even when you don't know, you can still ***project*** confidence and there is nothing controversial or objectionable about appearing confident. Amy Cuddy, Sheryl Sandberg and Valerie Young advocate 'fake it until you make it'. This philosophy has its supporters and detractors. Many people consider faking it to be the same as lying or being insincere and compare the term to 'bluffing', 'bullshitting', 'winging', and 'flying by the seat of your pants'. For me the trick has worked more times than I can think of. When I started off my career, in most public presentations I would be a quivering wreck, with my heart racing at an alarming speed. And yet, every time I would smile and speak up. In fact, in every event I made it a personal dare to myself to repeatedly step outside my comfort zone until speaking up started coming to me naturally.

You can start practising by speaking in smaller settings and gradually scale up. Psychologist Jenny Crocker has found that women thrive as 'we' and their confidence is twice as great when speaking for or advocating for a group or for 'others'. Hence, another way to build confidence is to start speaking on behalf of others.

Amy Cuddy's TEDx talk about 'power posing' has millions of views for a reason. She believes that power posing for a few minutes really changes your life in meaningful ways. She believes that our bodies change our minds, our minds can change our behaviour, and our behaviour can change our outcomes. In the same talk, she also reveals a study in which recruiters showed clear preference for people who appeared to be confident and displayed powerful posing despite being unaware of the background, hypothesis and conditions: "It's not about the content of the speech. It's about the presence that they're bringing to the speech."

Cuddy goes on to share the story of a Harvard student who told her she was not supposed to be there. Amy told her: "Yes, you are! You are supposed to be here! And tomorrow you're going to fake it.

You're going to make yourself powerful, and you're going to go into the classroom, and you are going to give the best comment ever."

Cuddy reveals that the next day that student actually made the best comment ever, which in turn made her classmates swivel in their seats and actually notice her for the first time. After meeting the same student a few months later, Cuddy realised that she had not just faked it till she made it, she had actually faked it till she *became* it.

Cuddy recommends faking it until we can internalise. She adds: "Don't leave that situation feeling like 'I didn't show them who I am'. Leave that situation feeling like 'I really showed them who I am'. Cuddy's TED Talk has benefited millions of people worldwide, especially women who have been socialised to 'fit in'.

The way we carry ourselves is crucial in determining our brand image in front of people. Are you comfortable in your own skin? When standing upright, what is your posture like? Is your spine elongated? Are your shoulders back and head held high?

When sitting up do you take up space? Do you wrap yourself in a ball with hunched shoulders, crossed arms and legs? Do you put both feet on the floor and open your chest? Do you sound confident? When meeting someone do you look them directly in the eye? Do you look self-assured? Is there an occasional lilt in your voice?

Eye contact, body language and facial expressions say a lot about you before you do. So pay close attention to them as you communicate with others. The good news is that all of these can be 'made up' to make yourself appear more confident than you actually are.

Beyond posture, it is also essential to speak up. My father always encouraged me to communicate with confidence and speak my mind, even if most didn't agree with what I had to say. He also emphasised the importance of being open to other viewpoints.

Public speaking runs in my family. My father, in particular, had no hesitation speaking to hundreds of delegates at various conferences, often spontaneously and without preparation. His speeches were entertaining and included a dash of humour. Even when he did rehearse, I would remember asking him: "What if you forget?" He said that it wouldn't matter given no one knew what his speech was about anyway. That was an important lesson to me. We are often afraid to speak up, and when we do, we are cautious about saying the wrong thing or even forget what we wanted to say.

My father used to tell me to never be afraid to disagree, but always be respectful and tolerant of what others think. He said that if you are good and you are right, you will be able to convince others. If not, they will convince you. "Remember, what is right should always be more important and bigger than your own ego. If you are wrong, never be reluctant to admit it." That's been my mantra ever since.

Speaking up is as important as the words we use. It's well known that women and men communicate differently. On average, women use nearly three times as many words as men to communicate verbally. Without a doubt, women include more exclamation marks, emotions and emojis in their written communication; they are often more expressive speakers too. I am quite guilty of that as well. Until recently, if I didn't add an emoji to my correspondence, it felt incomplete. Not only that, but when I replied to appreciative or congratulatory posts, I inserted every heart-shaped emoji I could find. I would even stop to check if I had inserted an equal number of emojis for every respondent lest someone get offended that they got one less. Yes, that's me. Guilty as charged!

Soon my emojis found their way to LinkedIn, Facebook, Instagram and Twitter. While I was always careful about sending heart-shaped emojis to professionals of the opposite gender, I inundated my female contacts with visual love. After reading an article discouraging their use, I realised how acute my problem was. No, I couldn't transition from excessive emoji use to no emojis at all.

What would people think? However, soon after I started using more formal communications, I noticed a big difference. Because others were so used to 'seeing' me communicate, they started taking me more seriously when I stopped using emojis in my emails. When I changed that, people started taking requests and comments more seriously. I have yet to work on my personal accounts.

If you share my emoji addiction, now might be the time to consider removing them from your professional emails because communicating confidence has a lot to do with the language you use. As Anna Wickham writes in her blog *6 Things Women Need to Stop Saying*: "It's not about the emojis, emoticons, and exclamation marks themselves. It's about the sentiment behind them. The next time you use a smiley face in a work email, consider why you wrote it. To soften a critique? To let the person know that you aren't angry for some reason? Try to figure out what you're trying to convey, then ask yourself whether you need to convey it."

It's not just emojis; women tend to use some words more than their male counterparts. These include saying sorry, overusing 'thanks', using the word 'just', or phrases like 'I think' and 'I was wondering.' These words and phrases diminish the importance of what you do and the recognition you deserve. They water down your authority at work and load your statements with ambiguity, leaving the misconception that you don't know what you're doing as a woman. It's a way of creeping up to a question and taking the edge off something directly.

Anna further states that men state their opinion as if it was fact, and so should we. Referring to our increasing use of thank you, she further points out: "There's an implicit gratefulness (for everything) present, even when the person on the receiving end is not doing you any favour in particular. Remember, no one is offering favours out of the goodness of his/her heart. This is work. You are doing your job. They are doing their job. You don't need to be apologetic or overly polite for asking for something."

In Tara Mohr's *How Women Undermine Themselves With Words*, she suggests avoiding the word 'actually' and other qualifiers that undermine our position: 'maybe', 'perhaps', 'I actually disagree…' 'I actually have a question', 'I'm no expert in this, but…' or asking 'does that make sense?' or 'am I making sense?' These phrases weaken your position before you've even stated your opinion. Admittedly, I often use these phrases, especially 'does it make sense?' when I want to confirm that I am on the same page as others. But according to Tara, this phrase comes across as either condescending (as in your audience can't understand), or it implies you didn't coherently communicate your thought.

Jenn Willey, my friend and training partner in the United States for Career Excel, an online woman's leadership programme launched this year, identifies vocal trends that women should abandon in order to be taken seriously. These trends include 'Valley Girl speak', Vocal Fry, Sexy Baby, Vocal Virus and low talking. As Jenn notes:

> "Vocal Fry is a vocal 'fashion trend' that is technically the 'glottalization' of your vocal chords, that results in a croaky sound, particularly as sentences are trailing off. It is a 'trend' that has been popularized in American culture by millennial celebrities like Kim Kardashian and Britney Spears.
>
> But this trend can be damaging to your professional image. Relative to a normal speaking voice, young adult female voices exhibiting Vocal Fry are perceived as less competent, less educated, less trustworthy, less attractive, and less hireable. What's more, women pay a bigger price for speaking with Vocal Fry than men; research shows that negative perceptions of Vocal Fry are more pronounced for female voices relative to male ones.
>
> Another type of 'vocal trend' impacting women more than men is 'uptalking'. This occurs when there is a rising intonation at the end of a sentence, so instead of making a statement, it turns into a question. To be clear – this is **not** about asking purposeful questions, but rather, a style of speech that consistently turns nearly every sentence into one

*that sounds like a question. Research reveals that women used 'uptalk' 1.5 times more than men, and more often when they were answering questions incorrectly. In fact, when they did **not** have the right answer, women spoke with 'uptalk' 76% of the time.*

In a Wet Cement survey of the 50 top male executives in the U.S. 4 out of 5 pointed to a lack of confidence as the biggest barrier holding back women in business today. That was followed by the need for more assertive communications. It's time for us to take back our voices and speak like the confident leaders we are."

It's not just about eliminating certain trends and phrases; it's about demonstrating that your opinion is valid, your viewpoint legitimate, your recommendations and thoughts are worthy, and thus you have the right to step up and speak. And you can do this by having your own style without the need to emulate anyone. By replacing meaningless and unnecessary words with words of value, you can change the impact of the entire conversation and how others perceive you. Fearless communication empowers your message instead of watering it down. It also helps you look confident even if you don't feel the same.

Refrain From Comparison

Comparison can be lethal. There are many famous people out there who are doing what you do and even doing it better, so why bother? You might as well not do anything at all. But this is not a justified comparison. If you don't measure up to successful people around you, that doesn't mean you are any less successful. Never compare other people's highs to your own personal lows. Remember, these highly successful people were in your place once. It may seem that some people achieve success effortlessly, but the reality is everyone faces a unique set of challenges and struggles only they are aware of. Learn to value your own strengths. Once you start respecting your own potential, you will soon realise that you have a lot to offer.

One of my LinkedIn contacts, Zeta Yarwood, a career coach and thought leader based in Dubai, narrated a beautiful story about her clients. I liked the story so much that I asked her for permission to include it in my book. Here it is:

> *"I have two clients: Samantha and Jessica. They are friends. Samantha is a successful businesswoman who spends much of her time travelling the world with her husband, staying in five-star hotels and flying business class. She also has a health condition which has left her overweight and unable to have children. Jessica is also married and a full-time mum to two kids under the age of four. She's physically fit and very attractive. Money is extremely tight in her household and, out of necessity, she freelances as a copywriter. She waits until the kids have gone to bed and starts work at 8pm, often not finishing until 1am. She's up again at 5.30am. Interestingly, both look at the other and think, 'I would love to have her life', neither truly understanding what the other one is going through."*

A few months back I shared my personal story when I was on *Feature Friday* of Trail Blazing Leaders. Here is what I said: "It's very important to note that every individual's journey to success and achievement has its ups and downs and must be undertaken with hard work, consistency and, moreover, resilience! You must be prepared to get up again and again and start from scratch if need be."

Many people have told me that I am lucky to be doing so well and achieving so much in such a short amount of time. Yes, I surely consider myself blessed. But for every achievement that I claim, there are several setbacks which you know nothing about. Why? Of course, I only publish my achievements on social media and not my failures so you only get to see the highlights of my life that I **choose** to show you and not vice versa. And this is precisely what most people do. They are not as comfortable and willing to disclose their disappointments and failures as they are sharing their successes!

For every article or interview published, or every victory of mine, there is a failed attempt, perhaps several, which preceded it. And you have no idea about those! If there is one thing I could share from my example or many others that I take inspiration from, that would be: *Success doesn't come easy and it certainly doesn't come overnight. So keep trying until you get there.* Here's my favourite quote from Nelson Mandela that sums everything up: "Do not judge me by my successes, judge me by how many times I fell down and got back up again."

Reconsider Your Perception Of Failure

Several women in my survey confessed that the reason why they don't try is because they know that if they don't try, they won't fail. I can understand where they are coming from. If you have been successful a number of times, the responsibility to continue doing well grows. As a role model and inspiration to others, that is not an easy pill to swallow.

The last few years of my career have been phenomenal. I've been fortunate enough to meet many wonderful women who told me that I inspire them. But inspiring others comes with responsibility. When people are watching you and drawing inspiration from you, you can't slack off. You have to go the distance because you learn to hold yourself accountable. You can't afford to disappoint. But then you must realise you are human and in doing so you give yourself permission to fail.

If and when you fail, you are motivating and inspiring others to a greater degree. Because then the people you inspire realise that they too stand a chance at success. Moreover, failure is important. It makes you stronger and teaches you much more than success ever will. We must also reconsider our perception of failure: it is OK to be wrong, to fail, to not know everything. Being wrong or unknowledgeable doesn't make you fake or non-deserving. Remind yourself that you will learn more as you progress.

Carol Dweck, a Stanford professor, introduced an important concept called the 'growth mindset' which really helps in recasting failure. A fundamental difference between men's and women's reaction to failure is that women consider their talents to be fixed, finite and immutable. Men, however, believe that they can learn almost anything. The growth mindset encourages hard work more than smartness. It motivates people to take up challenges and learn from them to enhance abilities. This in turn makes people resilient and more tolerant towards failure.

My mother-in-law is a savvy business woman of thirty years. She founded a school which grew to be the biggest and most well-reputed school in the area. At that time, and even today, it's a phenomenal feat. While we were discussing this book I asked her what her secret for success is. She shared an important insight which touched my heart; she attributes her success to her response to failure. She never gave up nor resisted taking risks. "Failure is a part of life so why be scared of it?" she added.

Top-notch teams sometimes lose, the best players often miss the goal, and there are many million dollar businesses that fail as well. Evaluate the impact of what could go wrong to mitigate your fear. Most importantly, reframe the failure as an opportunity to learn. Always remember, no one really knows the outcome. The fact that you are trying even when you are unsure makes you admirable and authentic.

Seek Out Coaching And Mentoring

Coaches and mentors help us realise that we may not be the best but we can get better. Coaches and mentors help guide you past obstacles and limiting beliefs so you can achieve your goals. They help you steer your way through confusion and overwhelming doubt so you can realise your potential. If you feel as though you need a navigator, consider hiring a coach to guide the way.

Pursue Your Goals Relentlessly

Pursue your goals relentlessly, regardless of how you feel; the best way to beat Impostor Syndrome is to continue taking action. It's been said that if you take the risk and do what you fear the most, then you can do anything. It takes a great deal of courage to pursue challenges even in the face of doubt. But you can never really know how much you can accomplish if you don't try.

I loved a story Danielle Macleod, co-founder of Somebody Inside, shared on LinkedIn. She's a friend and fellow coach who has pursued her goals relentlessly. She narrates the story of how she was offered a role she never dreamed of doing:

> "*I was the secretary made good, who fell accidentally into HR and then somehow ended up as director of a brilliant Change Management team. Miraculously no one had noticed that I didn't know what an analyst did... even though I had a team full of talented ones. I knew they were uncovering the detail, but they were way too clever for me. And now they were asking an ex-secretary already faking it in her Change job if she wanted to lead 10,000 people... Yes I do! But I didn't say it, not then. I went home and cried. My husband shook his head, 'This is the job you are made for!' 'I'm just a secretary inside. I've only got 65 people. I can't lead 10,000. They'll find out that I don't even know what Shrinkage means... (still don't). I'll say no.' I said yes. I loved that job. My team. Our people. We did amazing things. And there's still a bit of me that thinks now that I'm gone they've worked out I didn't know what I was doing... We've all got Imposter Syndrome. It's OK. Do it anyway.*"

Remember *Cars 3*? In it Sally Carrera wisely advises McQueen: "Don't fear failure. Be afraid of not having the chance, you have the chance!"

This was such a powerful statement. Not trying is worse than failing because you miss an important opportunity. When you refuse to try, you also refuse the opportunity to try, fail and learn from your mistakes. What's more, you refuse the opportunity to try and be successful! To endure without giving up, despite all odds, is one of the biggest lessons from the film. In my survey, many women revealed that they were risk averse. For example, Els Champer says having the stomach for risk has held her back in her career.

Here's the thing: as you look back on your career and life to date, do you ever wish you'd been a little braver, trusted yourself more, been less cautious to take chances? We are all innately risk averse, especially women. We are afraid of putting our vulnerability on the line. The status quo, while not particularly fulfilling, can seem like an easier, less scary option. I suggest you take that one action that creates a shift. And you can start by taking graduated risks. Remember, you can do one of two things: either change how you feel about the situation or change the situation itself.

Coping Strategies For Impostor Syndrome

Be Aware Of Your Feelings

Find Other 'Infected' People

Reframe The Context Of The Situation By Self-Questioning Limiting Beliefs

- Question Its Generality
- Question Its Authenticity
- Question Its Context
- Question Its Impact

Work On Self-Belief By Rewiring Your Brain For Success

- Express Your Goals Using Positive And Empowering Language
- Tell The Brain Exactly What You Want By Visualising The Outcome Using Sensory Words
- Link Massive Pleasure With Achieving A Goal And Pain With Lack Of Achievement/ Maintaining The Status Quo

Use The Brain Flip

Reaffirm Your Self-Worth And Own Your Success

Practise Confidence By Deploying Certain Strategies

Refrain From Comparison

Reconsider Your Perception of Failure

Seek Out Coaching And Mentoring

Pursue Your Goal Relentlessly

CHAPTER 4:

PERFECTIONISM

The essence of being human is that one does not seek perfection.

George Orwell

Perfectionism

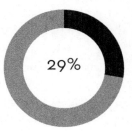

29%

Women around the world universally recognise perfection as one of their most difficult challenges to overcome. As women, our desire to do things perfectly is much more compelling than it is for men. However, the need to be perfect all the time can be exhausting for ourselves and for others around us.

Whether it's the appearance of ourselves, our children or our homes, whether we are working on projects or up against deadlines, we tend to go 'all out' in perfecting the details. We find it hard to delegate, as we believe others may not be completing the task as meticulously as we would. Thus we strive harder and put in extra hours to single-handedly shoulder the work of two or three people all at once. What's more, many women also believe that they are successful owing to the herculean efforts they put into their work, and hence they leave no stone unturned in executing their tasks.

Our thoroughness and fastidiousness breeds stress. And even though we need to ease up on our self-imposed pressures and deadlines, while learning to be more flexible, that's the last thing on our mind.

Women commonly hold on to the false notion that if they do things flawlessly, they can shield themselves from blame, judgment and shame. But holding up this heavy shield is what really prevents us from being seen.

Many people justify their quest for perfection by calling it a self-improvement tool. In reality, perfectionism has a lot to do with seeking approval, appreciation and acknowledgement. Most perfectionists have been brought up in an environment where they were praised for achievement and performance. Somewhere along the way, they consequently began equating achievement and accomplishment with quality of execution. In her book *Daring Greatly*, Brené Brown attributes this debilitating belief system to our upbringing: "I am what I accomplish and how well I accomplish it. Please. Perform. Perfect. Healthy striving is self-focused: How can I improve? Perfectionism is other-focused: What will they think? Perfectionism is a hustle."

Brené further clarifies that perfectionism is not the key to success despite what most people believe. In fact, research shows that perfectionism hampers achievement and is correlated with depression, anxiety, addiction, life paralysis and missed opportunities.

Before I delve into this subject further, I would like to introduce you to a certain type of woman – the Type A woman. It's absolutely critical to recognise the Type A woman because many of the challenges that follow are traits she typically embodies.

Raise Your Hand If You Are Type A

Type A women are typically hyper-focused and practically addicted to accomplishing goals. They have high levels of energy, are wired to keep busy and often multitask as a rule. Despite having impressive profiles, they still feel as though they have to achieve more in life. Type A women are also highly conscientious and care deeply. In all areas of their life, it's important for them to stay on top of things and ensure they execute everything flawlessly – whether it's planning parties or dinners, making loved ones feel special or completing projects. The downside, unfortunately, is that Type As find it hard to trust others, thus delegating is exceedingly difficult. They are sometimes considered impatient, controlling, overachieving perfectionists.

I know. I can relate. I am Type A too. Well, mostly! I am big on interpersonal skills and well liked amongst family and friends (or at least I'd like to think so). Yet when it comes to working as part of a team, I don't enjoy the same reputation. I have a very low tolerance for tardiness and incompetence. I am driven and goal-oriented, thus I am often more critical of others who don't share the same sense of urgency and thoroughness as I do!

You might already know that I run a *R&R Shero* podcast that interviews inspiring women making a difference across the globe. Last year I invited a very good friend and coach of Type A women, Jodi Flynn, to my podcast. We shared an interesting and entertaining conversation about Type A women. Right after my podcast, my inbox was inundated with messages from fellow Type As. Listeners thanked me profusely. One of them wrote: "You certainly described my personality as a Type A person and framed issues that have been part of my journey. It was an 'aha' moment for me to feel understood and honoured for both the ability to get things accomplished and [the] need to balance accomplishment with relationship building and self-care."

In my survey, women revealed that they often suffer from a severe form of perfectionism. Anne confesses to being a 'freakish perfectionist' and she feels bad about it, especially when it comes to her fiancé: "He can't seem to do anything right and I feel like a control freak and I feel like I need to loosen up but I can't."

Alicia says her biggest struggle is the inability to delegate. Kate shares that she wants to do everything herself because she is a perfectionist.

Perfectionism has a lot to do with social conditioning that starts early. Since birth, girls are subjected to a false ideology of perfection. These days young girls are increasingly concerned about how they look and how much they weigh. While it's good to watch your eating habits and live a healthy lifestyle, these girls are anxious to lose weight so that they will be accepted by society and avoid bullying. This is cause for concern. A government survey revealed that almost a quarter of girls between 8 and 11 years old admit they worry about their weight and appearance. As role models, we must encourage positive relationships and healthy habits. We must also counter the influence media has on portraying the ideal image.

It is up to us to teach girls that they do not have to be a certain weight or height to be successful. What they choose to wear and how they look has nothing to do with what they can achieve. Of course, I am not encouraging them to dress shabbily, but how much you weigh and how much skin you reveal should not have an impact on what you want to be or acquire in life. We need to show girls that it is OK to be wrong, to fail, to not know everything, because they can learn through experience.

Reshma Saujani, lawyer, politician and founder of tech firm Girls Who Code, delivered a powerful TEDx talk on how we have been conditioned to be perfectionists. In her story, she shares how she ran for congress when she was 33. This was the first time in her life that she had done something that was truly brave, where she didn't worry about being perfect or being alone. She talks about how girls have a 'bravery deficit', and that's why women are underrepresented in all walks of life.

She continues: "We're taught to smile pretty, play it safe, and get all As. Boys, on the other hand, are taught to play rough, swing high, crawl to the top of the monkey bars and then just jump off headfirst... We're raising our girls to be perfect, and we're raising our boys to be brave."

In the talk she shares a study conducted in the 1980s wherein psychologist Carol Dweck analysed how differently girls and boys addressed challenges. Despite having a higher IQ, girls were ready to give up while boys enjoyed the challenge and even redoubled their efforts. This study wasn't a question of ability but one of different approaches. Girls experience self-doubt despite routinely outperforming boys in all subjects. And this is carried forward. Reshma also cited the much talked about HP report that found men will apply for a job if they meet only 60% of the qualifications, whereas women will apply only if they meet 100% of the qualifications. She believes this study is evidence that women have been socialised to be overly cautious and aspire to perfection.

I loved the advice Mel offered in one of her weekly motivation *Take 5* emails after discussing Oprah's *60 Minutes* episode on childhood trauma: "So much of what happens to us in childhood impacts the adult we become. Instead of asking *what's wrong with me?* the better question might be *what happened to me?* Often the strategies you've programmed into your brain served a purpose at one time in your life. Are they still relevant today is the question we need to ask ourselves."

This is the question we need to ask ourselves as this question connects to our desire to be perfect, as well as many other socially conditioned challenges we face.

Coping Strategies For Perfectionism

Acknowledge That Done Is Better Than Perfect

Psychologist Tamar Chansky writes in her blog on perfectionism: "It's working with reality – with all of its mistakes, flaws, hiccups and wrinkles – that gives us the information we need not only to persevere, but to start again more effectively. This is how we succeed. So instead of concluding 'that didn't work at all!' we could think 'that didn't work yet,' or, 'some of that worked, and some of that didn't so what's my next step?'"

We have all heard the saying that on many occasions 'done is better than perfect', and rightly said so. There are some tasks that require a 100% commitment and output, for example, when driving, flying a plane or performing surgery. But not everything requires a perfect score.

As David Bayles says: "The seed of your next masterpiece often lies embedded in the imperfections of your current piece." Yes, the existing one with all its flaws. Too many people spend too much time trying to perfect something before they actually do it. Instead of waiting for perfection, run with what you know and fix it along the way.

The most dangerous way we sabotage ourselves is by waiting for the perfect moment to begin. Nothing works perfectly the first time because everything has a learning curve. We need to surrender our desire to do it flawlessly on the first try because it's not possible to have that perfect attempt. There is also a difference between obsessive perfectionism and healthy striving for excellence. There are certainly some areas where you can stretch to incorporate further improvements, but knowing when to stop is sometimes the more difficult challenge.

I loved the advice Michelle Green, author and teacher of *Business of Baking*, offered in my podcast: "I meet so many people who say 'Michelle, I can't start a business because my children are too young or I am too old, too short, too tall, too stupid, too broke, too whatever,' but I say, 'Oh gosh, please just start it, if you have a fire within you then just do it, maybe it will be imperfect, but better be imperfect and done than never done!'"

As Tamar says: "Don't Pull the Plug on the Project: Pull the Plug on the Perfectionist." Many business owners and authors advocate dropping the perfectionist hat. One of my author mentors was asking me why my book was taking so long to write. I explained that I was taking time to ensure that I had thoroughly researched and covered all points. He confidently asked: "Well, what are you afraid of? I make mistakes all the time, yet people still read my words. Enough said."

I was appalled. How could you make that kind of confession and be proud of it? But perhaps he is right. At that time he had already published five books and I was still researching my first one! If you wait for things to be perfect, you walk away with nothing. Sometimes we just need to jump in and get started. As David Burns points out, for women, perfectionism is a 'badge of honour' that leaves them playing the part of the suffering hero. And isn't that true?

Perfectionism is exhausting. Just to get a few moments of appreciation, we spend hours on excruciating details. Moreover, perfectionism can also be annoying and demanding for people around us, as Ze Frank says: "Perfectionism may look good in his shiny shoes, but he's a bit of an asshole and no one invites him to their pool parties." Though not sure why Ze referred to perfectionism as a he because I am pretty damn sure it's a she!

Be There In The Moment

Sometimes we are too focused on achieving results. When we only focus on the destination, we often forget to enjoy the journey itself.

I am a prime example of this. From dinner parties to birthday parties, from work deadlines to my son's school projects, I was often so obsessed with 'getting it right' that I often forgot to enjoy the actual experience. On the actual day of whatever event was transpiring, my face would be terse and I found it hard to smile. My friends hesitated to approach me because my stress was so apparent, I was snapping at everyone left and right! After thinking it through, I realised how inappropriate my behaviour was. I began to loosen up. I am still quite fastidious about certain things, but I have stopped fussing over tiny details that don't matter. Moreover, I make sure that I enjoy the preparation as much as the actual experience.

One of the major reasons why we aren't happy even after perfecting something is because we have not yet mastered the art of being in the moment. When we are home, our thoughts are still absorbed with solving challenges at the office. And we are so involved in yesterday and tomorrow that we never even notice that today is slipping by. If you cannot enjoy the journey, then why spend so much time pursuing it? Instead of relishing and living in that moment of success, people get busy setting up the next goal.

Reframe Failure

I have already emphasised the need to reframe failure in the previous chapter on Impostor Syndrome. I think it's useful to revisit Reshma's TEDx talk within the context of our perception of failure. In her tech programme, she instantly recognises her female students' fear of not getting it right, of not being perfect. Teachers at Girls Who Code routinely report to her the same story of how girls try, come close, but since they didn't get it exactly right, they delete the code and show teachers a blank screen. "Instead of showing the progress that she made, she'd rather show nothing at all. Perfection or bust."

She quotes the story of another friend who is a professor at University of Columbia. He revealed that when male students are struggling with an assignment, they'll come in and say: "Professor, there's something wrong with my code." The female students will come in and say: "Professor, there's something wrong with me."

Those are just a few examples from a popular TEDx talk. I personally know of and have heard of many more instances where girls and women have given in to second guessing, refused to raise their hands or stepped up. I share Reshma's belief that it is important to unravel the socialisation of perfection.

The reason we are afraid to fail as women is also because we tend to overestimate the probability of something going wrong, and exaggerate the consequences of what might happen if it does. We allow our misgivings to get the better of us. Rather than trusting our ability to mitigate the situation, we often conjure up images of things spiralling out of our control. Margie Warrell is a keynote speaker and best-selling author of *Stop Playing Safe*. She aptly shares our fear of taking risks and says: "We often conjure up images of ourselves shunned, destitute, shunned by our family, ostracised by our peers and forever shamed by our failure. OK, maybe I go too far. Maybe you don't catastrophise quite so dramatically. But the point is, we are neurologically wired to exaggerate how bad things could be if our plans didn't work out, and we fail to appreciate our ability to intervene to ward off further impact."

Shame is another reason we are afraid to fail. However, we must remember that perfectionism is not a way to avoid shame; perfectionism is a form of shame. And that element of shame is also stronger in women than it is in men. As Brené Brown says: "Shame feels the same for men and women, but it's organised by gender. Shame, for women, is this web of unobtainable, conflicting, competing expectations about who we're supposed to be. And it's a straightjacket. For men, shame is not a bunch of competing, conflicting expectations."

Take A Social Media Break

Steve Furtick said it best: "The reason we struggle with insecurity is because we compare our behind-the-scenes with everyone else's highlight reel."

Unfortunately, most of our negative comparisons often stem from social media comparisons. These activate triggers that can cause our self-esteem to take a sudden nosedive. As we've discussed, people use social media to showcase the best version of themselves, but not necessarily their authentic versions. Consider that many seemingly happy and successful people are more often than not battling hidden demons you know nothing about.

The desire to perfect our own lives especially intensifies when we compare our own not-so-glamorous realities to our contact list's ideal, perfect and filtered lives. A close friend of mine recently admitted that spending too much time on social media had plunged her into depression and caused her to develop a very low opinion of herself. What was interesting and rather sad was that the friend whose life she had benchmarked as ideal was actually struggling with an acute personal crisis, though her social media suggested otherwise. Many times we follow people we hardly even know or meet and create mental notes of standards these people keep so that we can strive to do the same.

Reducing your time on social media can make you less competitive and give you a much-needed break. Allow yourself only five to ten minutes a day to check your feeds. Resist rushing to pick up your phone with every notification. Life will be much better, I guarantee it! In particular, avoid looking at the profiles of people you routinely compare yourself to and use that time saved to redirect your focus to the things that really matter.

Avoid Gatekeeping

It's disconcerting to recognise that some of the time pressure we experience is courtesy of our own self-imposed high standards and expectations. One survey revealed this sobering detail: the majority of women respondents believed that if they did less around the house, they would feel as though they weren't taking care of it properly. An identical number said the exact same thing about the amount of time and effort they spent parenting. Women still feel that they are going to be held accountable if the housework and the childcare aren't taken care of flawlessly.

In some cases, women may be setting excessive and unattainable standards for themselves related to housekeeping and other family responsibilities. It's important to highlight the issue of control here. Women are quite sensitive about control, thus they are hesitant to relinquish authority and that in turn results in 'gatekeeping'. We want to hang on to things and not let go even if that means wreaking havoc in our daily lives. Home is typically considered a woman's domain, a place where we can generally set our own standards. Or as Susan Strasser, author of *Never Done: A History of American Housework*, puts it, home is a "sphere in which some women who have been denied power in other parts of their life have been able to obtain and maintain power."

In the same survey quoted earlier, 28% of married women frequently avoid asking their spouse/partner for help because they don't believe that their partner would do chores the way they would want them done. Many of the women from my own survey revealed they are hesitant to delegate home chores to their husband or partner as most feel that the tasks would be executed shabbily. Experts call this phenomenon 'gatekeeping'; women unwittingly prevent a more equal distribution of labour or even block a husband/partner's attempts to get more involved in housework or childcare.

Gatekeeping is a common phenomenon in Asian culture too wherein women want to be in charge of their domain and don't want to 'cede the power to someone else'. A 1999 *Journal of Marriage and Family* survey of 622 working mothers found that more than one in five could be classified as gatekeepers: "That group of women performed five more hours of family work every week than their peers did. What's more, many women refused any opportunity to outsource that work by hiring someone else to do it: 45% of respondents said that they would not hire more household help even if they could afford it. What's more alarming is that social media messaging reinforces this concept and often depicts women as inherently better homekeepers than men."

"Ads often convey the idea that women are inherently better at household chores than men," says Erica Scharrer, Professor of Communication at the University of Massachusetts, Amherst. Back in 2004, Scharrer studied commercials that were on air during a one-week period on primetime television. Of 477 characters depicted completing chores, 305 were women and 159 were men. Among the male characters, 50% were portrayed as comically inept. By contrast, more than 90% of the female characters were portrayed as competent. All household chores are typically portrayed as a source of pride for women."

A blog on Real Simple entitled *Why Women Can't Let Go* noted the aforementioned study and recognised that these types of ads have pervaded the airwaves for so long that they've penetrated our subconscious. "That may be the reason why approximately one in three married survey women said they were uncomfortable delegating household chores to their spouse."

Delegate

Don't waste your time doing things that somebody else can do, especially if they can do them better than you. The best professional is one who recognises the limitations of his/her competence. Save your time for those things that you are uniquely qualified to do. In addition to lightening your workload and making you focus on what really matters, delegating helps your staff learn new things and take risks while you are there for back-up if needed.

Similarly, do not avoid delegating tasks to your partner or even children. Make it a fun weekly activity. Before making the bed on weekends, my husband and son have a long monster fight and tear it apart. Moreover, my son is eager to do chores so that he can earn some reward points that will lead to a weekend treat. Some people might call it bribing – one friend even called it child labour – but I call it inculcating a sense of responsibility at a young age. And if he can do a few age-appropriate tasks at half the labour cost, then why not?

Often, people rise to the challenge when work is delegated to them. Delegating does not mean that you 'give away' work completely. As the owner of a task, you are ultimately responsible for the results achieved. If you are not in a leadership position at work, you may be thinking that you don't have anyone who you can delegate to, but that's often not the case. In many work teams, we can delegate laterally to a colleague who has a particular expertise, is looking for skill development, or simply has some extra time. At home, involve everyone in home activities as much as you can.

Decide Whether Perfectionism Will Add More Value

An important point to consider is whether spending more time perfecting something truly makes a difference or not. As a trainer, I would spend hours on fonts and templates until I realised that many of the best trainers had the simplest presentations. While you do need to follow some colour and design protocols to garner attention, some of the best training content I have ever used was minimalist in nature. In this case, spending more time on the content is more rewarding and meaningful than the design elements themselves. That brings me to the next important question.

How important is the project on which you are spending a painstaking amount of time and effort? When I planned parties, I would often spend too much time on minute details that didn't even matter. When I started attending other people's parties, I realised people had often spent much less time and effort on their event – so then why did it matter so much to me? I finally figured it out: it was because I liked doing it. I still do what I like doing, only minus the fuss and intricate details.

For us women, it is often an 'all or nothing' situation. As Tamar instructs: "Ditch the permanent score card. The pressure on the perfectionist is that every moment of stepping into the spotlight, every outfit, every lipstick choice, every word you write – from the note to the drycleaner to the editorial to the *New York Times* – is a moment with a permanent scorecard."

In any case, as we work to achieve perfection, time marches on, standards change, accomplishments are surpassed and the bar is set even higher. We are left more imperfect than ever, longing to achieve the next new standard of perfection. After all, perfectionism is a delusion that can rob us of a successful, enriching life if we're not careful.

Realise You Are Enough

Perhaps the most important aspect of perfectionism is to believe that you are enough. When we work from that place, we are not only kinder and gentler to the people around us, we're kinder and gentler to ourselves. Aiming for an error-free life is unrealistic and stressful. Do yourself a favour. Embrace imperfections and evaluate your life according to your level and parameters. Start from today.

Coping Strategies For Perfectionism

Acknowledge That Done Is Better Than Perfect

Be There In The Moment

Reframe Failure

Take A Social Media Break

Avoid Gatekeeping

Delegate

Decide Whether Perfectionism Will Add More Value

Realise You Are Enough

CHAPTER 5:
TIME POVERTY

The bad news is time flies.
The good news is you're the pilot.

Michael Altshuler

Time Poverty

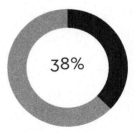

38%

Have you ever wished there were more hours in the day? More time to stay on top of your to-do list, pursue your hobbies, connect with friends, go out with your children for fun activities, and maybe even get to the gym?

You're not alone.

Women across the world are suffering from 'time poverty'. In my survey, a large majority of women, irrespective of where they lived, confessed that managing time was the primary challenge holding them back in their careers. Respondents ranked it the third highest challenge after FOMO and Impostor Syndrome.

To say that everyone is busy these days is an understatement, but if you're a working mum, spare time can be even more elusive. Women are certainly more 'time poor' than men. Research quoted in previous chapters clearly highlights that working mothers are more time starved than working men given their demanding schedules.

My husband's typical day involves waking up, showering, dressing, breakfasting, then travelling to work, working at the office the whole day, commuting home, playing with our son, eating dinner, watching television, listening to music and then sleeping.

My day involves waking up, showering, getting dressed, packing a lunch for my son, helping my son get dressed, dropping him off at school, tracking his progress, finding missing raincoats, hitting the gym (if time allows), coordinating with home contractors to fix things, returning home for breakfast, writing my blog, coaching a client or attending a training/workshop, networking, leaving in time to pick up my child, feeding him a snack, taking him to his extra-curricular activities, grocery shopping on the way home, staying in touch with family and friends, helping with school homework, doing laundry and washing-up, preparing a family meal (the last three tasks are often performed simultaneously), preparing our son for bedtime, getting his bag and uniform in order for the following day, preparing for my coaching or training session, spending time with hubs, reading a book and finally hitting the bed.

Now I am certainly not suggesting that my husband works less hard; in fact he works so hard that sometimes we hardly see him. Apart from extensive travelling and working late hours, he is focused on dry, often boring, number-crunching assignments that are much more exhausting than any task on my daily itinerary. And to be fair, he does help around the house and occasionally swaps duties as well. However, given the *wide* range of duties I perform *regularly*, duties that any other working woman has to perform as well, there is a constant pressure to maximise my time, which is only exacerbated by the desire to do things perfectly (please note: this desire doesn't concern men at all). That is what we call time poverty.

When compared to part-time working mums, full-time working mums have twice the workload and stress level. If you remove the mummy duties from this equation, life may be simpler, but it isn't any less demanding. Whether you are a mum or not, as a working woman you are still burdened with expectations of what you 'ought to' and 'ought not to' do. Managing work and home is still **your** responsibility and it's one that is traditionally passed on from generation to generation. Usually there is a tacit expectation for you to flex your schedule and realign commitments more than your partner needs to, or is required to do.

Completing our never ending to-do lists requires us to be hard-working, organised and efficient multitaskers as we play the role of multiple super heroes: 'Super Wife', 'Super Mum', and 'Super Professional'. The small break we might expect from our so-called 'downtime' isn't really a break at all as the laundry, rubbish, mail, pets and small children never stop needing our attention.

There are a myriad of tasks that rob women of their leisure time – from housework, to errands, to bringing up children. As a result, we are constantly running the time marathon and thus losing our opportunity to re-energise in our free time. In the Real Simple/Families and Work Institute (FWI) survey 'Women and Time: Setting a New Agenda', data showed that 49% of women say they don't have enough free time (defined as 'time that you spend on yourself, where you can choose to do things that you enjoy'). While nearly half of women manage to find 1½ or more hours of free time a day, 25% have less than 45 minutes a day, and 4% say they have absolutely no free time at all.

Melinda Gates addressed the issue with her husband, Microsoft co-founder Bill Gates. Specifically, Melinda calls out the gender disparity in time spent doing 'unpaid work' – work like childcare, grocery shopping and household chores. These kinds of tasks are the behind-the-scenes functions that keep people alive and healthy, while enabling society to function.

Her letter reveals that women worldwide spend an average of 4.5 hours per day on unpaid work – more than double the amount of time men spend. This type of work is historically undervalued and often taken for granted. These are also 24/7 responsibilities, requiring an on-call attendant at all times. In developing nations, the increased hours that women spend performing unpaid work translates into fewer available hours to pursue education, healthcare, and actual paid work that might help support their families.

The 2007 Time Use Survey (TUS), the first of its kind in Pakistan, revealed that women are more time poor than men regardless of whether the women are employed or not. This is due to certain women-specific activities that they have to perform irrespective of their employment status.

In more developed countries, including America, time spent performing unpaid work is less pronounced, but still highlights the disparity between how women and men live.

Melinda Gates' letter also underlines a noticeable gender gap relating to leisure activities. According to the Department of Labor: "The average American man will spend 73 more hours than his female counterpart participating in sports, exercise or recreation over the course of one year. He's not just getting more fit than her, somehow he's 'vegging out' more than her too. He'll spend 36.5 more hours watching television, and another 36.5 more hours participating in other leisure activities than she will. Across all data categories, men will spend more than 255 additional hours per year engaged in leisure activities than women will." The data also correlates with overall quality of life amongst genders. Women are twice as likely as men to suffer from depression, and twice as likely to suffer from sleep disorders as well.

Culture plays a role in time poverty too as it defines a woman's role in society and the nature of her responsibilities. From caring for children to running the household, being a working mother doesn't mean less of a load. There are no exemptions either. In fact working women are the most time-deprived category as they are expected to execute everything perfectly and have double the pressure. If they don't do that, they are shamed and ridiculed. In some cultures the social taboo is more pronounced, but the need to multitask constantly and its connection to time poverty is a global phenomenon.

Maria Shriver is a journalist, founder of *The Shriver Report*, and the former first lady of California. In her blog she writes: "For the millions of American women who live this way, the dream of 'having it all' has morphed into 'just hanging on'. Everywhere they look, every magazine cover and talk show and website tells them women are supposed to be feeling more 'empowered' than ever, but they don't feel empowered. They feel exhausted."

As highlighted earlier, the media plays a role in this too, often depicting women as inherently better homemakers and housekeepers than their male counterparts.

Erica from my survey shares that she is improving her time management skills so things are getting easier. But finding time for self-care is still quite challenging for her, especially since she works full time and runs a small business as well. As a paralegal manager who struggles with time management and works for three lawyers, Carol says: "In their mind everything is a rush! However their priority is usually not mine!"

Patricia believes she has already lost the battle to manage her own time and that procrastination has caused her significant disharmony, almost to the point of dysfunction. She is overwhelmed by too many choices, which leads to indecisiveness and the inability to prioritise. Anna recognises that because she overcommits, she struggles to manage her time.

Experts argue this point – although some household chores cannot be avoided, women are too mired in obligatory domestic duties and it's making them miserable. This is bad for their psyches, relationships and physical health. But I don't have to tell you that. If you're like most working mums, your life is likely choreographed down to the minute. That said, I can assure you that there are ways to master the fine art of 'doing more with less time'; even the busiest mum can carve out pockets of breathing room for herself on her most manic day.

Coping Strategies For Time Poverty

Is Multitasking Overrated? Do One Task At A Time

"Hira, you have only been in London for 21 months and you have been working on more projects than I have done in my entire career. You need to slow down and focus on one thing. What's your niche, anyway?"

This was the conversation I had with one of my mentors a few weeks ago. The phrase 'Jack-of-all Trades but Master of None' started ringing in my ears.

This is not just me; several Type A women have had similar conversations. Type A women are typically great at a number of things and are often equally as great at doing those things all at once. A few months back I met Alexandra Galviz, a very popular LinkedIn influencer and co-creator of LinkedIn Local. We immediately hit it off as we shared similar preferences and perspectives. She asked me to watch Emilie Wapnick's TEDx talk. After hearing what Emilie had to say, I realised I am not just a Type A woman, I'm also a 'multi-potentialite'. The next day my discussion with her was featured on LinkedIn and my blog on *Specialists versus Generalists* received a lot of attention.

'Multi-potentialites' share many symptoms with Type A women. They find it difficult to choose between goals because they have many different passions, interests and talents. As a result, these people are sometimes mischaracterised as indecisive or unfocused. At their core, 'multi-potentialites' are generalists rather than specialists – they are less focused on one particular thing and more focused on everything. Today, society tends to assign more value to specialists than generalists. But what if I have proved myself across multiple disciplines and am truly proficient at each? What if I don't want to be forced to choose just one?

In my LinkedIn blog on the above topic, I encouraged people to accept their multifaceted skillsets. I still do that today, in fact. I encourage women to pursue all of their goals, but that encouragement is based on one caveat: women should pursue those goals out of passion versus proficiency, ie just because you're good at something doesn't mean you're passionate about it.

What's more, just because you are good at a number of things doesn't mean you need to do them all. This last statement made by me when I was being interviewed for Jodi Flynn's podcast *Women Taking The Lead* turned out to be very popular and was tweeted many times. This interview itself had more than 2,000 downloads by women worldwide and women shared that they found this advice very useful.

We often take on many projects and assignments just because we are good at them, but often fail to consider if we are actually passionate about what we are doing. Passion matters on a personal level, but within the workplace you must also consider the business value of the projects and assignments you pursue.

If your goals and passions are already aligned, but you still struggle to stay focused, adjusting your perspective can help. My friend and fellow coach Sukaina once suggested that I stop thinking about my goals and plans on a horizontal timeline. That simple concept alleviates the anxiety of giving up certain projects today in favour of a future tomorrow. That advice has really helped me understand that I am not forever abandoning certain things, only postponing them. Focusing on one thing at a time also helped me find more time and reduced stress. People perform better when they give focused attention to the task at hand.

Survey respondent Michelle Minikinn suffers from FOMO so she tries to do it all. She sees opportunity everywhere – a fact which is both exciting yet draining. Coupled with lack of self-discipline, this makes it even more difficult for Michelle to maximise her time. By working with a coach, she soon realised it was more productive to focus on something now, grow it and systematise it, and then move on to something else: "I don't have to do everything now. I am gradually learning to streamline, automate and systemise," she adds. In addition, Michelle also benefited from the following strategies that helped her lose that constant feeling of being overwhelmed:

- Focus on what your values are – constantly question what you are doing. Does this opportunity live up to your values?

- Focus on Return on Investment/Return on Equity – does it need to be done now? Can it be put into the 'Ideas Book' for later?

Remember that no matter who you are or how talented you are, at any given moment you can only effectively do one thing at a time. Even when you are working on multiple projects and assignments, you can only give your 100% attention to the task in hand, and putting in more time on one task automatically means less time for another in any given day. Dan Gregory, author of the *Personal Leadership Training Guide*, writes: "Even a chess grandmaster playing 50 concurrent exhibition games at a big public event can only move one piece on one board at one time. Life is a series of choices, so choose wisely."

Prioritise

Michelle recommends completing a prioritisation exercise every weekend to help plan for the following week. Ask yourself: *What is urgent? What is important? What needs to be delegated? What decisions need to be made? What is pending? What can be put on hold for a week?*

- The Pareto principle, a concept originated with Italian economist Vilfredo Pareto, is often very helpful in prioritising. Relating the principle to time management means that 80% of your output could come from just 20% of your time, which can be achieved by frequently evaluating your tasks, continually assessing your goals, determining your prime time, and identifying as well as eliminating barriers.

- The Time Management Matrix by Stephen Covey is yet another very useful tool for prioritising. It involves four quadrants categorising tasks as per importance and urgency wherein: *Important responsibilities contribute to the achievement of your goals and Urgent responsibilities require immediate attention.*

- The four quadrants are: 1. *Urgent and Important;* 2. *Not Urgent and Important;* 3. *Urgent and Not Important;* 4. *Not Urgent and Not Important.*

- When using the Important-Urgent matrix, Stephen recommends to try to maximise the time spent with quadrant 2 activities. This will allow you (in the long run) to reduce quadrant 1 activities, as many of them could have been quadrant 2 activities if better planning had been implemented. It is recommended to avoid quadrant 3 and eliminate quadrant 4.

Michelle highly recommends the Pomodoro technique as well: estimate how much time an activity should take, then set a timer and try to complete the activity before the timer goes off. In other words, 'make a game of it'.

Embrace The Power Of Saying No

Let's stop for a moment and practise saying the word no together. Ready? No. *No*. **NO**. Doesn't that feel good? Don't you feel empowered? By its very nature, saying the word no gives you more control over what you actually say yes to.

Several women in my survey confessed that learning how to say no was a big challenge for them. Some avoid the word for Fear Of Missing Out. Some only say yes because they are multi-potentialities or Type A women. Then there are the 'people pleasers' – the women who can't say no because they are trying to make everyone happy all of the time.

Kimberly confirmed that Imposter Syndrome, lack of self-praise and perfectionism, have always been challenges for her. But the biggest is an inability to say no. "I have a tendency to people please, and am working on putting myself and what I need to get done first instead of other people's wants."

Trust me, most of the time pressures we face are connected to all the times we didn't say no. I'm still learning this myself. Many times when I have conceded to a request and said yes, I have ended up regretting it later. It wasn't until some of my projects fizzled out that I realised how relieved I was to remove them from my full plate. I was eager to finish those tasks I was passionate about, but I discovered that many others were actually unimportant and only added pressure unnecessarily.

Sometimes we do want to say no but we end up saying yes and this later becomes a source of regret and fatigue. So before saying yes, visualise yourself in that situation first. Are you excited or relieved that the event has been cancelled? If you answered yes, then that's a clear indicator to excuse yourself. And once you have said yes, don't give in to FOMO moments; focus on all of the benefits you realised by saying no!

Girl Boss's Sophia Amoruso's advice stuck with me: "My first reaction to almost everything in life has been no. For me to fully appreciate things, I must first reject them. Call it stubborn, it's the only way I can make something mine, to invite into my world rather than have it fall into my lap."

I couldn't agree more. Nothing will free up your time more than learning how to embrace the power of no. You don't have to attend every school meeting, chaperone every field trip or take on every additional work project. Stop being the 'yes' woman. Start training your brain to habitually say no, just like Sophia does. Proactively craft a few 'opt out' responses to favours or requests that you do not wish to oblige. Then rehearse those responses so you're comfortable actually saying them when the time comes to prioritise yourself.

By enforcing personal limits, you will also be teaching your kids the value of establishing boundaries. And while we are talking about boundaries, let's talk about an article I recently read entitled 'You Are Allowed To Have Boundaries With Family'. Natalie, the author, highlights some key and relatable points within. She notes there's nothing like family to bring out the people pleaser in you. What's more, she advises us to cancel our 'guilt account' and define boundaries – two critical tasks many of us women are unable to do. She suggests setting limits and clarifying priorities even if they seem trivial to others.

In the long run saying no can be an underrated but important key to happiness.

Set Short-Term Goals Then Break These Down Even Further

Break down your intangible dream goal into process goals that you can measure and deliver against on a controlled basis. That gives you traction towards your goals. Setting unrealistic goals and establishing self-imposed timelines only adds unnecessary pressure.

Ensure your goals are motivating and they stretch you. You can establish goals with *SPIRIT* (ensure goals are *specific,* have *prizes* attached, are *individual,* can be *reviewed* and are *inspiring* and *time bound*). In order to achieve your goals, add a task to your weekly to-do list that moves you towards your goals. Set three short-term goals you can work on one at a time. As you become more dedicated to the process, you can expand into five short-term goals per week. Next, map out the specific individual steps required to achieve that goal. Each step should have a deadline attached so you can continue moving towards your objective. Hold yourself accountable by committing to each and every deadline you set.

You can also employ visualisation techniques discussed earlier (thinking of the goal as if you have already achieved it) to help you realise it. In addition, consider creating a reward list. Rewarding yourself after each step helps you stay motivated and on track. According to David Allen, author of *Getting Things Done:* "We find projects overwhelming because we don't do projects, we only do actions related to them. And sometimes lack of time is not the issue but the lack of clarity and definition about what a project really is, and what the associated next action steps required are."

Develop An Outcome Frame

Once you have established goals and sub-goals, you are now ready to move on to the next stage: developing an Outcome Frame. All Neuro Linguistic Programming enthusiasts understand that an Outcome Frame is a valuable tool that helps give focus to your goals thereby saving you time. You can improve the likelihood of achieving your outcome by testing it from different aspects, and identifying resources you have or need. An Outcome Frame helps identify:

- The context for achieving the outcome

- The resources required

- The ecology of your outcome

- The desirability of your outcome

- The purpose of your outcome

- The process for achieving your outcome (how, when, what, why)

Always state your outcome in positive terms and base it on what you **do** want to happen and **not** what you want to **avoid.** Ask yourself these types of questions as you develop your Outcome Frame/Chart:

- What do you want? What else do you want?

- Why do you want the outcome? What values does it serve?

- What, where, when and with whom will you achieve this outcome?

- What are the internal and external resources required to realise this outcome?

- What specifically indicates you have achieved the outcome? What is the evidence?

- What will you gain or lose by achieving this outcome?

- What is your action plan?

- How will your monitor progress or deal with interferences?

Make Free Time Count

For working women, tiny blocks of 'bonus time' can be worth gold, and even a 15-minute window can feel like a hot minute. Productivity expert Carson Tate, author of *Work Simply: Embracing the Power of Your Personal Productivity Style*, recommends creating a '15-minute list' – a list of activities that can be completed in 15 minutes or less. This way you turn all that extra time waiting for coffee or the dentist into productive time you don't waste.

Carson also recommends that only action items should be on your daily to-do list, not the goal itself. Sometimes you just need to field the little things that reduce concentration and cause anxiety, like the clutter on your desk or a backlog of emails. This is the opposite of prioritising. Do the quick and dirty tasks **now**, even if you only do them for five minutes a day for the next two weeks. The crises in our lives are often the result of ignoring the little things or our own instincts; ie ignore the little toothache and wind up with a root canal.

Identify Your Energy Cycle

Are you a morning person or a night person? Everyone has specific times during the day when they are the most productive. When do you feel the most energetic, focused and productive? Identify that time to map out your day accordingly. The least liked and most difficult tasks should be done when you are most energised.

Carson Tate advises that we should determine our productivity type. According to Tate, most of us fit into four different productivity styles:

1. **Arrangers:** they think about their projects in terms of the people involved

2. **Prioritisers:** the definition of 'goal-oriented'

3. **Visualisers**: they possess a unique ability to comprehend the big picture

4. **Planners:** they live for the details

Tate believes we can leverage these four cognitive styles to more accurately and effectively help us in stop being busy and start being productive.

Distance Yourself From The Net

We can use our email as a personal assistant, as it helps us both filter and prioritise. However, too much social media can be our undoing. Surfing the web is a huge time waster; an innocent little break can turn into hours of wasted time you can't get back. Turn off notifications that distract you from completing your tasks.

Browsing social media leads to sleep deprivation too. Establish limits on screen time for yourself and your kids, then unplug once you've reached that limit. Tate tells us not to start our day with email because we are reacting to everyone else's to-do list instead of working through our own. While it's certainly important to reply to emails as a responsible professional, only your personal to-do list includes steps towards achieving your own goals.

Get Organised

Productivity research indicates that the average person spends about 10% of the day looking for things. Doing the maths, you could gain five weeks a year just by getting your retrieval methods under control! If you tend to keep track of things at work, consider things at home. Do you have a place for your keys, glasses, or lunch bags? Do you ever find yourself searching for things in the morning right before you leave for work? How long does it take you to find a particular file on your computer? (This is one of the most common time suckers out there!)

Did you realise you can save yourself an hour each day just by getting organised? Take time to put things in their proper place at both work and home. Use your workspace and personal space (home, vehicle, garage, etc) to their greatest advantage. There is no need to do a big clean-up once a year if you can take a half hour once a week to file, sort, and put things in their place. It is important to identify and operate within two time horizons: short term and long term. Anticipating events will help you to get things done in the short term and achieve long-term objectives.

An up-to-date master calendar and a 'Things to do today' list helps focus attention on the highest priority items. Action planning worksheets, milestone charts, and PERT project management diagrams are excellent planning aids as well.

Additionally, throw out or take home all those things you have collected at work that you don't need or use. We're so used to holding on to things that we're sometimes afraid to throw out the wrong thing. Use the same rule at work and at home; if you haven't used it for a year (or an entire business cycle), get rid of it, because you obviously aren't using it.

Sort and group things you use. Your desk should be organised logically: pencils and pens in one place, another place for letterhead and envelopes. Have a basket for projects and another one for priority items so that you can locate the things you need when you want them. You can use the same kind of system on your computer so that you can find your working files. Once a project is complete, move it into an appropriate folder for retention. In short, set up a system that works for you.

Know That There Is No Such Thing As A Perfect Balance

While we talk a lot about balance, we often fail to accept that each day will not be perfectly balanced. Some days we will do nothing but put out fires, but those crisis days are balanced out with days that are quieter when the phone isn't jangling off the hook. You can also achieve balance by setting your work aside and taking a brisk walk at lunchtime or phoning someone that you care about. Achieving balance is not necessarily about spending equal time on the things you like versus things you don't; it can be about the value of things. A big smile and a quick lunch with someone can balance out a morning spent in a frustrating meeting.

Get Enough Sleep

Prioritise your sleep needs so you can thrive. You'll drag all day and ultimately waste time if you're under-rested. Schedule sleep like any other activity and go to bed at bedtime so you can function the next day (enforce your kids' bedtimes too, it's good for all of you).

Establish Sane Work Hours

Before you commit to a new role, make sure your expectation of work hours aligns with your potential employer's. Life commitments and job projects will ebb and flow, so check in periodically to ensure expectations remain unchanged. That way, if your boss typically calls or emails after hours, you can decide whether you're available or not. Many working mothers reserve nights and weekends exclusively for family.

Let Go Of Perfection

It doesn't exist, therefore you can't achieve it. Instead of obsessively cleaning an already clean-enough house, or toiling towards intangible ideals (like being the 'perfect' mum or having the 'perfect' figure), identify a more practical use for your time and have some fun along the way. Stressed-out people aren't all that productive. You need relaxation to avoid burnout at home and at work. Make time for holidays, long weekends and family fun to keep you grounded and joyful.

Be Present

Mindfulness allows you to tune into the task at hand. Yoga or meditation can help you focus, and focus drives productivity. Embrace the method that speaks to you, and tune back in when you catch yourself drifting.

Stop Owning Other People's Stuff

How often do you hear yourself saying, 'Never mind, I'll do it myself?' Probably more than you'd like. We all tend to take on more than our share of responsibility and it's a real time waster. The solution? Let others manage their responsibilities themselves. This includes your children, spouse/partner and colleagues.

Let Go And Delegate

Learn to know when to let someone else handle a task. Relinquishing control is tough, but it's also necessary to allow others to pitch in. Delegating is not admitting defeat. Rather, it's maximising the potential of your entire network.

Stop Procrastinating

Women are seen to procrastinate often because it provides us with a built-in excuse to shield us from the fear of failure. When we don't try or finish, how can we fail, right? Well, I have already talked about the importance of failures, so if that's the reason then ditch the habit of delaying.

Brian Tracy wrote a great little book called *Eat that Frog!* In it he quotes Mark Twain: "If the first thing you do each morning is to eat a live frog, you can go through the day with the satisfaction of knowing that is probably the worst thing that is going to happen to you all day long." Mark Twain also suggests if we have two frogs to eat, to eat the ugliest one first as comparatively the rest of the day will feel like a breeze. Another good way to counter procrastination is to delegate, prioritise and create deadlines as soon as you get them.

Coping Strategies For Time Poverty

Do One Task At A Time

Prioritise

Embrace The Power Of Saying No

Set Short-Term Goals Then Break These Down Even Further

Develop An Outcome Frame

Make Free Time Count

Identify Your Energy Cycle

Distance Yourself From The Net

Get Organised

Know That There Is No Such Thing As A Perfect Balance

Get Enough Sleep

Establish Sane Work Hours

Let Go Of Perfection

Be Present

Stop Owning Other People's Stuff

Let Go And Delegate

Stop Procrastinating

CHAPTER 6:

SELF-PROMOTION

*I would venture to guess that Anon,
who wrote so many poems without signing them,
was often a woman.*

Virginia Woolf

Self-Promotion

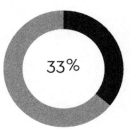

33%

One of the most difficult things for women is self-promotion. Anything that remotely hints at self-aggrandising will have women run a mile.

I moved from Dubai to London and started my business from scratch in the process. The one factor responsible for my success and growth in London is self-promotion of my brand. In Dubai, I remained relatively unknown, but I lived a comfortable tax-free life and had a steady base of recurring clients. All that changed when I moved to London. I had to start all over again and I didn't know where to start. My husband suggested I start blogging, podcasting and networking to make a name for myself amongst a large global audience. Wasn't he smart? That recommendation worked wonders for my career and helped me in establishing my own personal brand with an entirely new audience. Within 18 months I was published 26 times across global publications like *HuffPost, Thrive* and *Women@Forbes*.

Soon I was invited to various forums, conferences and podcasts. But being published and interviewed wasn't enough; I made sure to negotiate a valuable deal every time I was published, featured and interviewed. That, in turn, had a cascading effect, but initially it wasn't easy.

Self-promotion is synonymous with bragging out loud and that's tough for women to do. It makes most of us exceedingly uncomfortable; before people can start making assumptions about you, you start assuming the worst yourself.

But hear me clearly: *There are some things you've got to do!* Remember the first time you changed your baby's nappy? While some mothers find even this duty adorable, I definitely wasn't one of them. But you get me, right? It wasn't the best experience but you still did it because it needed to get done... not just once but every... single... time. Self-promotion is pretty much the same. It's not just a one-time activity. You need to do it again and again until you get comfortable, and then you do it some more. Ever wonder why celebrities are so active on social media? They're already insanely popular so why do they have to keep showcasing their brand? Because in today's landscape it's more difficult to get your message across. There are lots of choices available and attention spans are short, so you really need to shout out loud if you want to get noticed in the crowd.

As a recent study at Montana State University confirmed, women have a hard time speaking up when it comes to their achievements for fear of sounding arrogant or conceited. Men, on the other hand, don't share this problem. While women feel uncomfortable touting their own success, men see self-promotion as a positive trait.

Peggy Klaus, author of *Brag: How to Toot Your Own Horn Without Blowing It*, says that the entire notion of self-promotion is excruciatingly difficult for many professionals to embrace, even if they know it is critical for their own survival. "So ingrained are the myths about self-promotion, so repelled are we by obnoxious braggers, many people simply avoid talking about themselves," writes Klaus.

Briana from my survey asks: "Am I bragging? Or just standing up for myself?" Meredith says networking/relationship building and highlighting her own accomplishments are her biggest challenges at work. Beth admits that it's challenging for her to accept praise. Susan and Anteje feel the same.

No one is asking you to be a braggart when tooting your own professional horn. Practise humble confidence, but do not shy away from self-publicity and shining a spotlight on your achievements, especially those that promote your brand. Being too humble can cost you. Failing to point out your accomplishments can hit you in the wallet. "It's those who visibly take credit for accomplishments who are rewarded with promotions and gem assignments," writes Klaus. Self-promotion is even more important in today's less stable job market. "Even if you aren't an entrepreneur," says Klaus, "you need to think like one and start talking up your most valuable product: you." If you want to learn how stepping up to showcase your services can lead to astounding results, wait till you hear about Jevaani, son of my mentor and friend Carol Stewart; LinkedIn UK's Top Voice. Jevaani is the same young man who created quite a national stir when he handed out his DJ card to Prince Harry and Meghan. That one act of boldness landed him several opportunities later on.

Moreover, our stories reveal our true selves. When we share stories about our accomplishments, we reveal our true selves. It is only through revealing our true selves that we break through superficial small talk and make real connections, form genuine friendships, and deepen our relationships.

Coping Strategies That Make Self-Promotion Easier

Think Of Yourself As A Brand

The best way to address this is by considering yourself a brand. This way it's not about you, but the brand you represent. Companies brand themselves to create an image. We create a personal image for the same reason – to build a brand around ourselves that leads people to think of us in a certain way. When we refer to 'your brand' in this respect, we're referring to the **package you want to offer others**. It is a reflection of the story you want to tell about yourself and how you prefer others to see you.

Building a brand is crucial as it precedes your reputation and is the first step in creating a rewarding career. It opens doors for you, generates new opportunities, and lends you greater credibility. It's also a way to construct the right kind of footprint for yourself so that you can provide people with content that bolsters their opinion of you. When designing your brand, ask yourself the following questions:

- What is your existing brand like? What are three words that describe you?

- What is it you do that makes you, or your work, stand out as special in other people's minds? Whatever the *stand-out factor or specialty* is, it becomes part of your personal brand.

- What do you want people to think of when you network with them, sell to them, interview with them, consult or help them?

You can even solicit feedback from colleagues, team members or clients. Based on the answers above, formulate your own personalised brand statement. Remember the key is to focus on highlighting those points you want people to remember about you and resist including everything that you have ever accomplished. Be specific. Be distinct.

Once your brand is specifically tailored and purposefully designed, start afresh and simply start behaving in those ways you identified in your brand description. Focus on where you want to be with your new brand and not where you were prior to developing it. By having a plan to follow, you will feel less cautious of the process and more focused towards the outcome.

Sallie Krawcheck, Chair of *Ellevate Network*, recommends testing your brand with your personal board of directors before formally communicating it to ensure that you are right on track.

Lastly, book an official launch and celebrate the new you publicly by setting up a marketing plan to purposely promote your brand. Caroline Dowd-Higgins, author of the book *This Is Not The Career I Ordered*, says: "Take Your Power – power is not given, it's taken, so create your brand and project it out into the world loud and clear." In order to publicise your new brand, you need to start self-promoting in a way which is consistent with your brand image. Identify behaviours and actions that can lend credibility to your brand.

Sometimes people are too conditioned to perceiving you in a certain way, so it may be difficult to relate to the new you. That's understandable given you are changing and they are not. If you're serious about rebranding yourself in a specific way, then you need to expand your network to include new people who never knew the old you and don't have to be convinced. Remember, it's not about you anymore but the brand you represent! Stay focused on proactively choosing how you promote yourself. After all, your professional brand is your responsibility – manage it judiciously!

Document Your Successes And Achievements

This list is invaluable when it's time to ask for a pay rise and/or promotion. This record serves a twofold purpose: first, you can consult it when you encounter self-doubt as it is a reminder of your on-the-job successes; second, you'll be prepared with an accurate record of all the great things you've accomplished for your company when the time comes to review your performance and compensation.

State Facts As They Are

Own your achievements without overdoing it. It's important to be concise in your explanation, stating the facts in a simple, direct manner. Self-promotion backed by evidence to substantiate it is well received. This conveys confidence and authority versus arrogance.

Give Credit to Others

Giving the rest of the team due acknowledgement and using 'we' instead of 'I' is a good rule of thumb to avoid coming across as a narcissist. Be sure to highlight and thank 'the team' for valuable accomplishments as you articulate your own personal contributions.

Accept Praise Gracefully

When you are recognised for your accomplishments, do not shrug it off. Many women love using the phrase 'Oh, it was nothing.' Remove this from your dictionary! As noted, recognising team effort is important; however, reporting your accomplishments with pride and giving them the due importance is even more crucial. Accept your star role in your own production. Downplaying your involvement doesn't help build your brand – it damages it. A sincere thank you and a firm handshake shows you appreciate acknowledgement of a job well done.

Use Social Media To Your Advantage

We've devoted considerable time to the negative effects of social media so now let's recognise how you can use it to your advantage. Social media tweets and posts can help leverage, shape and strengthen your brand (assuming it's appropriate for your job). Be smart and selective – share information that defines your brand interests and expertise, not undermines your professional reputation. Sharing and commenting on topics that showcase your brand is another valuable way to build awareness for yourself. You can even volunteer to write for your company newsletter or any professional organisations that you are a member of.

Tell A Story

If you are reluctant to share a personal accomplishment, try weaving it into a story form. It always helps and is definitely more memorable too. I remember the first time I delivered a training to 50 policemen in Pakistan. It was a pretty cool, badass thing to do and I was proud to share that experience with others. Although I trained an even bigger audience a few months later, I was hesitant to share that accomplishment. My brother suggested sharing my experience as a story so I could shift the focus to my presentation content, the area challenges where I was training and the participants themselves. And that's exactly what I did. That simple change of approach helped me feel more comfortable talking about myself because it was less directly about me.

Show Vulnerability

Showcasing achievements by sharing your struggles and sacrifices along the way is always an engaging way to help people relate to and learn from your experiences. People love heroism. And it makes you human too – a genuine and relatable one. Inspiring stories that have a zero to hero angle always resonate well. By re-telling how you survived and overcame a challenge, you make your story authentic and motivating for others around you. Such stories give hope, and hope can be a very powerful thing. Owning your mistakes and sharing them honestly can also help you build solid relationships with your team.

Be Grateful For Your Success And Show Humility

I have underlined the importance of owning success and saying thank you when others compliment you. But accepting your success and bragging about it are two different things. No one likes braggers or thankless people who take all the credit for themselves. Have you ever heard award speeches in which celebrities thank all the people responsible for getting them there? It's one thing internalising your success and knowing that you had a role to play in it, more than anyone else. But it's another thing to say that out loud without recognising all of the people who helped make you successful along the way. There is something about humility and expressing gratitude that makes people more agreeable. Humble leaders are in tune with their teams and are often the most well-liked and respected leaders as well.

Use Self-Deprecating Humour

One study discovered that frequent use of self-deprecating humour was linked to a better overall psychological wellbeing. When you hear someone make fun of themselves, you usually assume that they're doing so to conceal their insecurities. However, according to a recent study, this is often a tactic some of the most popular leaders and influencers employ to make themselves more relatable. When you are your own comedic target, you also tend to be happier and more self-assured. Self-deprecating humour often minimises status distinctions between leaders and followers. It also makes you more likeable. So when you are out there self-promoting, don't forget to inject a healthy dose of this type of humour. By laughing at yourself, you ensure others have a stronger desire to support you because they're laughing right along with you.

Recruit A Wingwoman

In the book *Reinventing You*, author Dorie Clark suggests bringing a friend along to events where you may need to talk about your accomplishments. The author suggests making an arrangement with the friend that you both will 'talk up' the other. Thus, instead of bragging about your own experience and background, you boast about your friend's and they brag about yours. "People you are speaking with are much more likely to be receptive to a third party bragging about you than if the information was coming from you personally (even if you're standing right there, giving your best 'aw shucks' grin)." Also, women are often found to be far more confident when advocating for others. Some people even advise making use of the 'buddy system' in which your colleague or team member promotes and nominates you for awards and you do the same for him or her!

Keep Mini Elevator Pitches Handy

Elevator pitches are typically succinct and persuasive sales pitches about yourself, your experience and/or your offerings. These speeches take the same time as an elevator (lift) ride, hence the name. John Corcoran, an attorney and former Clinton White House writer, also refers to elevator pitches as 'brag bites' that are short sound bites or brief marketing monologues about yourself that you can use at a moment's notice and in any situation. Endow these intros with energy and enthusiasm and practise using them. By preparing them in advance you can ensure that you don't come across as pushy or disingenuous when an opportunity arises to extol your virtues.

Don't Share All Of Your Achievements At Once

You want to give the person you are talking to just enough so that you are memorable and interesting, but not so much that they are overwhelmed. Space out your achievement announcements.

Nobody wants to see your achievements splashed all over their social media profiles, not even your biggest advocates.

Well, at least not every other day. There have been times when I have received consecutive PR successes in one month, but I stopped myself from sharing them all at once. Firstly, it gave me real news to share during quiet months when I had nothing else to promote; and secondly, I did not want to overwhelm people with one accomplishment after another. Like it or not, people get tired of seeing someone else's perfection broadcast on a regular basis. Moreover, sometimes when meeting new people, the last thing you want to do is bombard them with useless information that doesn't leave an impression. Work in your accomplishments where they naturally fit, rather than forcing them into conversations just to brag.

Coping Strategies That Make Self-Promotion Easier

Think Of Yourself As A Brand

Communicate Your Brand

Document Your Successes And Achievements

State Facts As They Are

Give Credit To Others

Accept Praise Gracefully

Use Social Media To Your Advantage

Tell A Story

Show Vulnerability

Be Grateful For Your Success And Show Humility

Use Self-Deprecating Humour

Recruit A Wingwoman

Keep Mini Elevator Pitches Handy

Don't Share All Of Your Achievements At Once

CHAPTER 7:

VULNERABILITY

Only when we are brave enough to explore the darkness will we discover the infinite power of our light.

Brené Brown

Vulnerability

18%

Lately, workplace vulnerability has been recognised for its role in creating cultures of trust, engagement and respect. As leaders, being vulnerable means that we no longer need to hide how we're feeling – we can own it while being attuned to our own emotions and the emotions of others. Importantly, vulnerability also entails bearing the discomfort that comes with exposing your emotions. It means we do not need to outrun or outsmart uncertainty, risk and emotional exposure. We need not be the expert all the time; we can ask questions when we need answers; we can ask for help when we struggle; and we can ask for feedback when we are actively working to become the best version of ourselves. What's there not to like about vulnerability?

Many leaders embrace vulnerability as it allows them to connect with colleagues and team members on a deeper level. Leaders who admit to shortcomings while admitting that they do not have all the answers are able to spark open dialogue with colleagues and team members. People at work feel closer to them as the team can share candid feedback without hesitation. This, in turn, fosters a collaborative environment. Vulnerability evokes trust. After all, there is something relatable and likeable about people who show their softer side. People who are open to admitting mistakes or shortcomings, or make fun of themselves, make us feel like they are one of us.

Vulnerability also allows leaders to be more creative as people can take more risks and experiment with new ideas when they are less afraid of being exposed or ridiculed. Moreover, another strong argument in favour of vulnerability is if no one really knows the authentic you then you might avoid fundamental relationships in life. By not allowing yourself to be completely open with people you love and care about, you are actually hurting yourself.

In the long run, vulnerability enables your relationships to thrive and endure. If people leave you at your most vulnerable moments, perhaps they are not meant to be with you. In short, research supports that vulnerability is the birthplace of love, belonging, joy, courage, empathy and creativity.

But the important question remains: should women embrace this in their work life or not?

This is one challenge that did not reveal any definitive answers because respondents were divided on the issue. Some women said it helped them, while many others believed their vulnerability had held them back in their career.

The Reed Smith, We Are The City report on high achieving women, *The Art Of Success*, also revealed that the one question around emotions had truly divided opinion. In response to 'Is there a place for emotion in the workplace?' the research found a 50/50 split between those wishing to rein in their emotional side (including sensitivity and passion) and those who felt they should not hold anything back. The report suggests that given this existing generation is far more in tune with their emotions, it might be time for all of us to tap into our emotional intelligence more.

Best-selling author and social scientist John Gerzerma notes this: "Our research shows that what people describe as traditional feminine skills and competencies are requisite for sustainable success in the modern era. In our global survey, we found that 79% of people are more open to showing their feelings than in prior generations, while 81% agree that today's times require we be more kind and empathetic to others." After surveying 64,000 individuals in 13 countries, John's thesis found that traditionally feminine leadership and values are now more popular than the macho paradigm of the past. Despite these overwhelming statistics about the importance of vulnerability, how you manifest it in the workplace is far more complicated.

A *Girl Guide* blog refers to what is commonly known as the 'messy middle' of the professional pipeline where women fall off in middle management. According to the report, amongst other things that are lacking such as wage gap, employee development and work-life balance, is support, which is irrefutably linked to vulnerability.

Vulnerability is typically considered a weakness, hence we as women will do anything we can to avoid the appearance of not being 'strong enough'. As women, we are constantly encouraged to hide our softer side or keep our feelings to ourselves. As a result, most women are really quite good at masking their emotions, don't you think? The truth is that being vulnerable is scary for even the most confident women. By exposing how you really feel or think, you are opening yourself up for people to see into the person you truly are, which most people don't want to 'risk'.

However, as we step into our power, it is important to accept vulnerability rather than avoiding the authentic you. Even though being vulnerable can feel dangerous and unsafe, it will never compare to that nagging feeling of 'what could have been' when you leave important words left unsaid.

One of the world's leading researchers on authenticity, Dr Brené Brown, discovered one of the critical components for great leadership is the willingness to be vulnerable with others and 'failing big'. She shares that vulnerability is often gender defined. With millions of views, Brown's TEDx talk in which she describes her transition journey from not accepting to accepting vulnerability is one of the most popular of all time. "Both women and men could benefit from allowing themselves to be vulnerable. I think vulnerability and shame are deeply human emotions, but the expectations that drive shame are organized by gender. For women it's 'Do it all, do it perfectly and never look as if you're working very hard' – which is a disastrous set-up. And for men it's 'Don't be perceived as weak'."

Dr Brown also notes that vulnerability is difficult to embody as it's the first thing we want to see in others and yet the last thing we are willing to show. Brown believes there are three shields we use to protect ourselves from vulnerability: perfectionism (doing everything perfectly); numbing (using alcohol, drugs, food or work to deaden true feelings); and 'foreboding joy', the dread that kills happiness. She argues that we should drop those shields. She discloses that when she visits corporations she encounters as much resistance to vulnerability from female leaders as male ones.

And it is true; sometimes vulnerability can backfire even when leaders have the best intentions. One of my friends landed a promotion, then told her new team that she wanted the job but it was scary, so she elicited the team's support. Her full-disclosure, seemingly authentic style of leadership caused her to lose credibility with her employees.

Given the challenges women face, it comes as little surprise why women are naturally inclined to bottle up and resist exposing weakness. My own survey indicated somewhat similar results. Whereas women in the western world had mixed opinions about how vulnerability impacted their career, 90% of Asian women believed that being vulnerable held them back. And in a culture where women already struggle for the simple right to work, vulnerability becomes a question of survival. Therefore, it becomes necessary for them to wear a cold mask of indifference and show undeterred courage even in their weakest moments.

Some survey respondents shared that being vulnerable on the job backfired for them. Cathie reveals that she used to be more passive and polite, but a male manager once told her that working in tech meant she had to be tougher with the men she worked with. "Best advice I ever got. Not rude, just more pushy."

Gretchen shares that she got a bit teary-eyed in an interview when describing a previous career decision that had a negative impact. Afterwards, she was told that she did not get the job because she was emotional. What's more, the interviewer was another woman she knew professionally, prior to the interview!

Survey respondent Sally doesn't think she has shown much vulnerability, although she is sure it's there! Janet feels it's hard to know if vulnerability is a positive or negative because most superiors don't tell you they fired you because you were too vulnerable. She recalls a situation in which she was laid off because she was in a vulnerable position owing to a messy divorce and crazy ex-husband.

HR super heroine, and my Pakistani friend and partner, Maheen Noor Soomro, thinks there were very few times in her career when she showed vulnerability. However, the one important time she did, it was because the balance in her life was toppling (due to several personal and relationship/family issues). Unfortunately, that one time she was vulnerable with a select few she considered her mentors, they used it against her. "It just made me wary of trusting people or choosing the people I wanted to really depend on."

But then there were others who were in favour of showing vulnerability. Nancy shared that being vulnerable has "helped me feel and be seen as more authentic and trustworthy."

My coach and mentor Jenny Garett, an inspirational woman and author of the book *Female Breadwinners*, shares the story of her amazing client whose home was damaged by fire. She was living in a terrible situation for more than a year, but never mentioned her personal trauma to her team because she didn't want to burden them. After some coaching, when she did decide to open up, she was surprised at the support she received and how willing her staff members were to go that extra mile and also be more open about their own difficulties.

Mandy revealed that until she was able to embrace her vulnerability it was a pain in the a*** and that her career really suffered because she could not request help or make mistakes. Jenna believes that you must be vulnerable or you will not grow. Kat says vulnerability has helped her. "Lack of vulnerability has hurt me in my career. Openness and admitting when I need help, especially, has been very important. Trying to do things myself and not being vulnerable has bitten me on the backside."

Amy Matos said: "I fully embrace vulnerability. It's not easy, but I think it's important to building trust, especially in an online forum."

Maheen shares that although vulnerably didn't always help, there were occasions when it did, especially when she was exploring new terrains. Showing her vulnerability made some of her mentors she has learned from come out and help her in innumerable ways.

They could see that she was struggling and offered help themselves. She still respects them and has great relationships with them.

Interestingly, a few women believed that being vulnerable has really helped them grow their own business even though it didn't work so well in their careers. Along these lines, Leah Garvais says: "This is such an interesting question. It did not help me in my 9-5, but it's the only reason starting my own business has worked and has grown. Such a contrast!"

Lina admits: "To be honest, I suppressed the vulnerable part of myself for such a long time being in a male-dominated industry. It hasn't been until recently, with my own business, that I started to open up. I feel blessed to have known both sides of the coin to be honest. I believe honesty with oneself is what's most important. Now, I can decide if I want to be vulnerable or not, depending on the situation."

Tash Pennant helps people connect with brands and organisations from the inside out through effective internal communications. This is her experience:

"The ability to be vulnerable has been a struggle because I worried about what others would think of me or if their perception of me would change. So I recall one day in winter 2017 I woke up and wrote my first 'Just so you know' post on social media which poured out some of the challenges I faced. As I wrote it, I was crying because I felt I was losing face. However, the number of private and public messages I received was overwhelming and heartening in support of my disclosure of challenges I faced. Being vulnerable allowed people to see that there was relatability in some of the same obstacles others experienced. I had them too." As Tash says: "At times being vulnerable is a plus and enables people to relate and connect with you."

Being vulnerable in the workplace is tricky for many women, especially if they are already seen as strong leaders. But the core question remains: as strong, capable women, how do we prevent ourselves from being 'professionally incarcerated' for doing anything outside our restricted social norm without being considered 'weak' and 'emotional'?

Even though many men experience depression and other health conditions, these are typically not attributed to their gender. With women, however, these issues are almost irrevocably linked to their gender, creating an automatic divide. Women who fail to meet society's standards for appropriately expressing emotion are labelled too intense and too angry.

In an article entitled *Women & Emotional Vulnerability*, writer Anna Leksa confesses that she sometimes adopts an "unflattering traditionally masculine handling of emotions," but she says there are cultural reasons why she navigates the world this way, as for women competing in "what is so obviously a man's world" it is difficult to admit to stress and overwhelm. They act invincible and see exposing emotions as "too much of a risk."

It is difficult to achieve the perfect balance between sacrificing authority and being iron-fisted. And that's when most women are still struggling between the need to be liked and not needing to be liked. Unfortunately, neither approach is effective in a long-term leadership position.

Coping Strategies That Will Help You Be More Vulnerable

Develop Self-Awareness

Building self-awareness or developing self-leadership is key to becoming more attuned with your emotions and feelings. Self-awareness involves developing a sense of who you are, what you can do and where you are going coupled with the ability to influence your communication, emotions and behaviour on the way to getting there. Increased self-awareness can help you realise what you value and what you need. You can start off by documenting those emotions in a diary to help identify feelings and triggers before you break down. Here you might want to go back to Chapter 3 where this process has been explored at great length.

Meditation, mindfulness and breathing are great tools for developing self-awareness. Brené Brown recommends figuring out what our 'armor' is: "Are we hiding our true selves behind perfectionism? Intellectualizing? Cynicism? Numbing? Control? While this armor feels like it's keeping us safe, it's actually shielding us from the chance to feel truly worthy of connection. We can never really guarantee the outcomes of anything we achieve, so instead of putting on a mask of perfection and concerning ourselves with what people will think or say, why don't we allow ourselves to be truly seen as someone who is authentic?"

Develop A Strong Sense Of Self-Worth

In order to be comfortable being vulnerable, you need to believe you are worthy enough. If you are cautious of your actions and how people will react consequently, it becomes difficult to express yourself truthfully. Brené Brown explains this in her TED Talk: "There was only one variable that separated the people who have a strong sense of love and belonging and the people who really struggle for it. And that was, the people who have a strong sense of love and belonging believe they're worthy of love and belonging. That's it. They believe they're worthy." Love and appreciate yourself first, and the rest will follow.

Strike A Balance

Most women leaders who I admire have struck the right balance between confident executive and collaborative leader. You risk losing credibility and respect if you are too professional (no one gets to see the real you), or conversely if you overshare. Get to know your team while also setting clear boundaries and expectations.

Professional behaviour and authenticity must go hand in hand. Women tend to gravitate towards a more casual and collaborative leadership approach. However, that approach can be undermined by overly personal behaviour. On the other hand, an authoritarian method is not better either, as it fosters fear and blame, thereby compromising creativity and risk-taking. I have personally struggled to achieve this balance. I tend to be overly friendly with team members and clients, which makes it harder to be stern when performance is at issue. This sudden change in behaviour didn't go down too well with many people; and in the beginning of my career, some team members even started calling me moody!

Identify The Root Cause Of Your Existing Behaviour

In his documentary, *I Am Not Your Guru*, Tony Robbins asks one of his event attendees this pivotal question: "*Who did you crave love from most as a child, and who did you have to be to get it?*"

Sometimes the person you thought you had to be as a child in order to feel fully loved and accepted is the very person you are still trying to be in adulthood. And sometimes, that doesn't work because what you pretend to be is not actually who you are inside. What's more, trying to be someone you're not over the long arch of your life can be both painful and exhausting. Perhaps it's time to dig into the past, discover why you act a certain way, and reframe your future behaviours in a way that is true to yourself.

Consider How Lack of Vulnerability Is Impacting Those Around You

Jenny Garrett shares her powerful story of transformation in one of her weekly blogs. She shares that in the beginning of her career, she was dressing older to fit in and was using language that wasn't her own to disguise who she really was. It was only when someone pointed this out to her that she recognised how her behaviours could damage her otherwise strong sense of self. Can't we all relate to Jenny in this regard? Remember how I wanted to colour my hair white?

Jenny then went on to share how this experience made her realise the potential impact this behaviour may have on her daughter. As a result, she chose to embrace her differences rather than hiding or denying them. By doing that she was in turn giving others permission to do the same. She felt liberated by the concept.

Sometimes how we influence people around us really makes us revisit our choices. I too, like Jenny, strongly advocate embracing differences. My son is a third culture kid, and despite the many advantages that brings, being in that category has its own set of challenges. The least I can do is to encourage him to express his authentic self and be proud of it. I tell him, just as my father once told me, that there will always be someone who doesn't believe in what you do or what you say. And you know what? That's OK, because learning how to effectively express yourself in the face of scepticism or criticism will help build your character. Develop the courage to be your authentic self, no matter what others think. After all, authenticity and vulnerability go hand in hand; you can't really be authentic unless you choose to open up.

Trust Yourself To Handle The Outcome

When you choose to be vulnerable, others might not accept or appreciate it. People might reject you or desert you. Some may even respond harshly, but if you keep things in perspective – ie make it a point to accept all of that negativity with a pinch of salt – then you will always emerge stronger no matter how extreme the reaction. You need to trust yourself enough to withstand any criticism or opposition in the face of vulnerability. If we believe that we have the emotional strength to calm our temporarily jangled nerves, we will be able to confront our vulnerability with courage and determination.

Let Your Feelings Out

If you face rejection in the face of vulnerability, do not bottle it up and hold back your feelings. That one rejection should not determine your future course of action. By sharing and venting to someone you trust, you will feel better, potentially 'lighter', and likely restore your own faith in open expression. Leon F. Seltzer says: "It's important to keep in mind that depending on others to soothe us can actually *increase* feelings of vulnerability."

Remember That Vulnerability Makes You Stronger, Not Weaker

Jennifer Kass, from the self-development site *Mind Body Green,* explained: "It's only when we close our hearts and put up protective barriers that we are at the mercy of everyone and everything around us; from this place we become victims of our circumstances and give away our power by letting external things and other people control how we feel."

By not being vulnerable, you give others the power to hurt you. Thus if you *really* want to protect yourself from being hurt or emotionally bruised, then become more vulnerable. According to Marlen Komar, when we show our vulnerable side, we give ourselves a 50:50 chance of achieving a happier, more meaningful life, which is infinitely better than having no chance at all.

In *Daring Greatly: How the Courage to Be Vulnerable Transforms the Way We Live, Love, Parent and Lead,* author and PhD Brené Brown said this: "I can honestly say that nothing is as uncomfortable, dangerous, and hurtful as believing that I'm standing on the outside of my life looking in and wondering what it would be like if I had the courage to show up and let myself be seen. Don't jip yourself a shot at being happy. Open yourself up and see what happens – contentment might just be on the other side."

Coping Strategies That Will Help You Be More Vulnerable

Develop Self-Awareness

Develop A Strong Sense Of Self-Worth

Strike A Balance

Identify The Root Cause Of Your Behaviour

Consider How Lack Of Vulnerability Is Impacting Those Around You

Trust Yourself To Handle The Outcome

Let Your Feelings Out

Remember That Vulnerability Makes You Stronger, Not Weaker

CHAPTER 8:

MANAGING STRESS

I've yet to be on a campus where most women weren't worrying about some aspect of combining marriage, children and a career.

I've yet to find one where many men were worrying about the same thing.

Gloria Steinem

Managing Stress

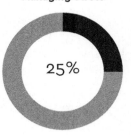

25%

The World Health Organization recognises stress as the 'Health Epidemic of the 21st Century'. Eight years ago as a leadership trainer for a multinational pharmaceutical company, I developed a programme to address this growing epidemic. I called it 'De-stress & Revitalise Your Soul', and exclusively dedicated it to women in my company. The programme later became an annual flagship event and to date it remains one of my most popular training sessions with clients. Despite its popularity, I am often asked: "Why only women?"

First, as a woman myself, I relate more. Second, as already reiterated several times in the book, I firmly believe that women juggle multiple responsibilities at once, more often than men have to, and are hence more susceptible to stress. It's not only about multitasking; in any given day working women are required to run a 'multitrack mind' as well, rapidly switching between different tasks across various roles. Managing both work and home is a responsibility traditionally passed on to us, and, as highlighted earlier, there is usually an unsaid expectation to flex our schedule and realign commitments more than our partner needs to or is required to do. The juggle is real.

According to *Harvard Business Review*, women experience more stress at work because, on top of domestic responsibilities, they must also contend with a stereotype threat at work – a phenomenon unknown to men.

I'm not sure where I read it but this quote says it all: "It's hard to be a woman... you must think like a man, act like a lady, look like a young girl, and work like a horse."

Dr Daneim Amen has found differences in female and male brains. He found that female brains are more active in almost all areas, especially in prefrontal cortex and limbic cortex. One study suggests that women have 30% more neurons firing at any given time than men. This indicates strengths including empathy, intuition, collaboration, self-control, but also makes women more vulnerable to anxiety, depression, insomnia, pain and being unable to turn off their thoughts. The worrywart centre, the amygdala, is definitely found to be larger in women.

The Confidence Code on several occasions cites how the female brain works differently from the male brain: "We really do have more going on, we are more keenly aware of everything happening around us. And that all becomes part of our cognitive stew." The book also reflects on how women "spend time in overthinking and undermining themselves with tortured cycles of useless self-recrimination." Unfortunately, the propensity to ruminate is not selective, and applies to our personal and professional lives and relationships equally. This tensile capacity for brooding, routinely feeling inadequate and taking blame for others, among many other traits, often leads to anxiety and depression.

The right kind of stress, also known as positive stress/eustress, can be beneficial as it can challenge and motivate us. However, it is usually bad stress/distress that we fall victim to. The good news is that there are many simple ways to minimise the negative impact of stress. These revitalising stress-busters when practised regularly can make bad stress a thing of the past!

Coping Strategies For Stress

Find Reasons To Be Positive And Grateful

I often emphasise the importance of gratitude in my leadership trainings, particularly in trainings that are focused on resilience and stress. Gratitude is that one habit that can make all the difference in your daily life and can be a powerful weapon against heartbreak. It's a practice that can eliminate half of your stress straight away. Negativity and unhappiness are as contagious as happiness, positivity and gratitude. When you are grateful, you attract positive energy all around you and vice versa. However, do not confuse gratitude with acceptance towards your status quo or being lackadaisical towards goals. You can be grateful yet still be ambitious and demand what you deserve.

Negative feelings sap energy and set up a self-perpetuating cycle of disappointment, worry and regret. Waking up each day and acknowledging just one positive thing, and the less obvious blessings, goes a long way towards recuperating the most dampened spirit. Gratitude journals are a great way to help you do this. They also encourage calm, lowering stress levels and granting new perspectives. When regularly pursued, this type of writing can prove to be an effective stress-busting activity in itself. Also, often authentic confidence manifests itself the strongest where there is positivity, high self-esteem and gratitude.

My mother taught me the importance of staying positive and expressing gratitude, even in the face of adversity and heartbreak. Many years ago, I distinctly remember how her one response triggered my journaling habit. I was feeling despondent so I called her for comfort and solace like I usually do when I find myself breaking down or giving up. She said something very powerful to me that day, something that has stuck with me ever since:

"You know, Hira," she said grimly, "you have a lot of things to be grateful for in your life and let me remind you, you got most of these things without even asking. So if you can be blessed with things that you never really imagined nor prayed for, then how is it possible that God will not give you the things that you are praying and longing for? Of course He will, just have faith, wait for the right time and continue being thankful." Her words stirred my soul and got me thinking. It's true – pain easily overshadows joy; we are quick to point out what isn't working in our lives. What is going well, however, takes time to recognise, because it's likely something we commonly take for granted. And this is exactly where gratitude journals can help. They remind you to take into account all of the good things in your life and set your day off on the right foot.

Yes, there are times when unanswered prayers make us stressed and heartbroken. But what about the many other times when we are blessed beyond measure, bestowed with blessings that we never even asked for? These blessings might seem pretty ordinary to us, but they may mean the world to someone else.

Remember, every day you have a choice. The choice to wake up happy and content or to wake up complaining, complaining about what you don't have enough of, whether it's money, opportunities, love, respect, etc. If you choose to focus on what you don't have, then that's how your life will play out: it will never be enough and you will always be seeking more. However, when you are thankful for the countless blessings that you do have, that's how life will be for you: content and happy.

Set Attainable Targets

Break long-term goals into small attainable sub-goals or steps. This has been explained in the earlier chapters. Reward yourself after each step to stay motivated and on track. Breaking down your journey into smaller milestones then celebrating them along the way will give you a sense of purpose on your road to achievement. Who doesn't like celebrating every now and then, anyway?

Don't Forget To Celebrate Life's Little Moments

My parents love celebrating – whether it's festivals, events or people themselves. There is nothing they like more than making loved ones feel special. They have always encouraged us to be warm and courteous so we could share the happiness and sorrows of others. I have seen my parents heartily reciprocate generosity and thoughtful gestures, often giving in return much more than they received. Acknowledge your friends and family members for their achievements and successes. It's equally as important to acknowledge their pain. This is an ideal way to eliminate stress. Great leaders are there for their team during crises, but they are also there when it's time to celebrate team achievements and make their people feel special.

Laugh Heartily And Often

Laughter is the best therapy out there. Moreover, it's free! It gives your heart and lungs a good workout, and research indicates that laughter releases feel-good brain chemicals which in turn lower blood pressure and relax the muscles while reducing pain and stress hormones.

Spend Time With Loved Ones

Spending time bonding with loved ones over coffee/lunch or even a Skype chat provides emotional support and distracts the mind from the daily grind. Take time to enjoy your children – play with them, act silly. Their enthusiasm and vitality will rub off on you. Plan nights out or lunch dates with a friend. Hire a babysitter and go out and have fun with your spouse/partner. Better yet, if you are like us, stay in, cook a lavish meal, snuggle up and watch a film. You will never feel more relaxed!

Schedule Breaks From Time To Time And Take That Holiday

The other day my husband and I were discussing how rarely he takes a sick day from work. This might be a good sign, though I refuse to believe that out of 365 days there isn't a single day he can take off to rejuvenate and re-energise (after all, prevention of sickness is important too, right)? What's more, how about annual holidays? I know many people who are afraid to take those because they will miss work! Seriously!? What have we come to?

Not long ago I woke up in the morning feeling exhausted. I am generally a happy and motivated person who is passionate about her work. But during that period, I was waking up secretly hoping for assignments and projects to be cancelled or postponed. For a person who loves her work, this was surely a sign that I needed to disconnect and take a break (or learn to start saying no).

I therefore decided to reprioritise my goals. This was followed by spacing out self-imposed deadlines and making a conscious effort to unwind every day, primarily by closing my laptop an hour before dinner. Most businesswomen can relate to the issues an unpredictable work schedule creates. Yes, we can be more flexible with our time. But on the other hand, we can continue working non-stop as we often work from home without any commute breaks. Some people recommend sundown as a 'down time' for yourself as well, at which you shut off, completely disconnecting from work and social media.

Meet New People And Network

My family passed on the art of networking to me. Despite being an extrovert, I was not particularly comfortable networking until I started running my own businesses. That's when I realised how important it is to make meaningful connections. My dad always made it a point to meet new people – in our own country and in every new country that we travelled to. As a result, we have established lasting friendships with people from various faiths and cultures, all around the world.

Networking can be beneficial not only for your career but your overall wellbeing too. Meeting new people can be a refreshing change and can really open up your mind. It can lead to new opportunities and new potential ways to work together with new contacts.

Nurture A Hobby

Invest time in doing something you enjoy such as painting, cooking or anything that excites you. When you spend time doing something you are passionate about, you invigorate your soul and feel an inner sense of satisfaction and contentment that even therapy can't give you. Sally Hubbard from the *Women Taking The Lead* podcast, suggests making time to find joy: "Mark time off your calendar for joy and make it a priority that you schedule everything else around."

Your hobby doesn't necessarily have to be something big. It could be spending time on something small and meaningful. A while ago, I did a series of webinars to mark the launch of Career Excel, a Women's Leadership Programme I run. Kalyani Pareshi, a motivational speaker, and I jointly hosted one such webinar on coping strategies to overcome personal and professional challenges. Kalyani focused on emphasising the controllable factors in our life versus the non-controllable ones. I especially loved this advice of hers regarding turning ordinary things into extraordinary that can lead to instant gratification and a boost in self-esteem. She shares an example:

"Let's start with cooking; I have always made the same things over and over, not really changing things up, so I looked up recipes online and started making new dishes and I got instant gratification when my family appreciated what I cooked up. I took something as ordinary as cooking and made it extraordinary. The idea behind it was to show to myself that I can take on something new and succeed at it, it was to enable me to believe in myself again."

Take A Break From Social Media

I know this is the third time I'm offering up this strategy, but we can solve so many of our problems by simply distancing ourselves from social media. We have developed an unhealthy psychological dependence on our phone which adds to our stress and robs our time. We are not just addicted, we are trapped. I am so much more productive on the days I don't log in at all. One chapter from Arianna Huffington's book *Thrive* is titled *Your Smart Phone Isn't Making You Wiser*. In it she notes that one of the things that makes it harder to connect with our wisdom is our increasing dependence on technology.

She further adds that: "Our hyper connectedness is the snake lurking in our digital Garden of Eden. Technology has made it possible for us to live in a self-contained, disconnected bubble twenty-four hours a day. Our devices may seem that they are connecting us, and they do to a degree, but they are also disconnecting us from the world around us. And without being connected to the people we encounter, it's hard to activate our hard-wired instinct for empathy."

Arianna recalls the time she broke down. When compared to traditional measures of success focused on money and power, she was very successful but she was not living a successful life by any sane definition of success. "I knew something had to radically change. I could not go that way," she writes in her book *Thrive* and quotes this from Rumi: "You wander from room to room hunting for the diamond necklace that is already around your neck."

Meditate And Practise Mindfulness

Take 10 to 15 minutes each day to just sit by yourself and let your mind float. Meditation declutters the mind, helps you unwind, develops an inner sense of calm and equilibrium, and boosts your mood. Mindfulness helps you focus on the present moment rather than worrying about the past or dwelling on regrets. It enhances your ability to control your emotions. Indulge yourself with a luxurious warm bath or light up some scented candles, close your eyes and let your mind and body drift. What's more, meditation and mindfulness also shrinks the fear centre in your brain – the amygdala.

Minimise Decision Fatigue

Every morning you wake up you have decisions to make. By some estimates we make 35,000 decisions every day. No wonder we feel emotionally drained by the end of the day. After making all these decisions, the mere thought of making another one is exhausting. People often find themselves depleted and overworked, and it's not lack of coffee!

Roy F. Baumeister, social psychologist and author of *Willpower: Rediscovering the Greatest Human Strength*, identifies the culprit as 'decision fatigue'. One way to minimise this is by establishing daily routines that minimise decision-making, such as wearing the same outfits. There are many advocates of the style repeat movement like Arianna Huffington and great leaders such as Steve Jobs, Mark Zuckerberg and Barack Obama. By developing this routine for menial tasks (like getting dressed) these leaders conserve brain space and energy for larger decisions. Arianna is of the opinion that men have a competitive advantage over women because they don't stress as much, or spend time thinking about, buying new outfits.

From time to time, taking the much-needed break and pulling back your brain from chaos improves its neural connections, thereby enabling better decisions. Perhaps that's why our best ideas come while we are in the shower or taking a stroll?

Treat Yourself Once In A While

Retail therapy is overrated. I would opt for spa therapy any day. If you want to spend money, go to the salon and pamper yourself. Manage your finances and treat yourself with a massage, facial, manicure or pedicure. Or if the spa isn't your thing, then treat yourself to something you enjoy, something that stimulates you. It doesn't have to be expensive – think cycling/walking/swimming/canoeing in a peaceful setting. Restaurants, cinemas, spas and entertainment places frequently offer amazing deals. Look out for them and book yourself a treat depending on what takes your fancy.

Exercise

Any form of exercise, whether it's dancing, yoga, walking, or even daily stretching at work will make you healthier. What's more, you don't have to spend a lot of time doing it. Even just 20 minutes of an activity you enjoy is enough to improve circulation and kick starts your metabolism in the right direction.

Just Feel Good: Anytime, Anywhere, Always

Don't let the weather or anything else as trivial negatively influence your mood. Be in charge of your own happiness and always look forward to the good that is yet to come. It's OK to fret and panic. It's OK to vent out too. It's also OK when your superhero cape gets tangled up with stress, but when it does, just take a break to untangle it, breathe in deeply, lift your chin and continue marching forward with your cape flying nice and high. P.S. Don't forget to breathe out.

Coping Strategies For Stress

Find Reasons To Be Positive And Grateful

Set Attainable Targets

Don't Forget To Celebrate Life's Little Moments

Laugh Heartily And Often

Spend Time With Loved Ones

Schedule Breaks From Time To Time And Take That Holiday

Meet New People And Network

Nurture A Hobby

Take A Break From Social Media

Meditate And Practise Mindfulness

Minimise Decision Fatigue

Treat Yourself Once In A While

Exercise

Just Feel Good: Anytime, Anywhere, Always

EXTERNAL CHALLENGES

The biggest obstacle I have had to overcome
is being a woman in a man's world.

Zoe Saldana

External Changes

CHAPTER 9:

MALE-DOMINATED INDUSTRIES

In my survey and trainings, women have increasingly pointed out how difficult it is to climb the corporate ladder in male-dominated industries that reek of misogyny and male privilege. Women's low employment within some fields correlates to negative perceptions of workplace fairness and personal treatment. It's not much fun being the only 'type' in the room, whether it's owing to your gender, faith, background, orientation or preferences. The experience can be alienating and takes a toll on your self-esteem and performance. You may also have to deal with discrimination or the pressure of tokenism. Tokenism involves hiring women as a display of supporting diversity. But that in itself can lead to a lot of pressure as you are expected to represent your minority group, and the responsibility to prove yourself can appear to be enormous. When we are part of a minority in an institution, and that minority has a well-known stereotype about performance already associated with it, we feel pressure to confirm to that type. This leads to increase in consciousness of what people may think and battling of assumptions, even if they are unconscious and implicit.

Research has evidenced that women speak 75% less when men are in the majority. They have no qualms in asking questions in front of other women, but in male-dominated audiences, women struggle. Moreover, women that have risen into leadership positions report that the expectation around their performance was beyond that of their male counterparts.

Furthermore, as Lois Frankel states in her book, rules, boundaries and strategies are different for men and women and people of colour. The boundaries are widest for men and narrowest for people of colour. Boundaries also vary from company to company and boss to boss. As a woman, it's important to size up the playing field of the company you are working in and decide if it's you or the size of the field holding you back.

All of that said, there are many strategies to help women survive and thrive in more challenging work environments. Many of the strategies have been taken from my blog published in *Forbes* on minority women.

Coping Strategies To Succeed In Male-Dominated Industries

Understand That Not Everyone Will Open Up to You

Sometimes, difference in preferences leads people to exclude you. A man's behaviour often changes when he's with other guys, and their sports talks may not always sound inclusive. Unfortunately, not everyone will overcome their reservations despite your best efforts. No matter how well intentioned, not everyone is aware of female nuances, thus risk coming across as ignorant or condescending. While this is not an excuse, the truth is that most people tend to work with tunnel vision, only seeing what's directly in front of them versus what's beyond their narrow perspective.

Avoid Isolation And Communicate

You may need to find ways to reduce being isolated. Identify common bonds with co-workers. When there are fewer women in a meeting or boardroom, they are often viewed as outsiders. To overcome this barrier, it is critical to seek out ways to bridge the gap and identify shared interests. Help others understand that you might not fit the stereotypes that society defines for most people in your group. Get to know them as people. Ask them about their families and hobbies. Deep down we are all human beings and have similar drives. The people sitting across the table from you are human. They have their own fears, dreams and experiences. In this age of radical transparency, open communication is critical to removing these barriers and better understanding your colleagues. When you truly understand your colleagues, you can develop authentic relationships with them. Sometimes all it takes is communication and awareness.

When Alicia from Comsat switched to a new job, she constantly felt pressured and often found herself wondering about what would be the next 'trick' up her sleeve. Her new boss did not invite her to dinners. Instead of sulking, Alicia chose to confront the issue by carefully working this into a conversation with her new boss. Alicia believes that it's all about creating awareness and communicating concerns in a subtle not awkward way.

She recalls the time when she wasn't offered a role because her boss wrongly assumed the more demanding nature of the role might not suit her as 'a woman'. Alicia later addressed this issue when she answered a diversity study question about what it was really like to be a woman. She explained to her boss how important it is for colleagues to treat women working in the office as team members and professionals first, and women second. She made her boss realise that women must contend with incorrect assumptions and inappropriate questions on a regular basis. That valuable exchange was eye-opening for her boss. Effective communication can change future behaviour in positive ways. When her boss had an open position and a qualified pregnant employee, he asked her if she wanted the role instead of assuming that she wouldn't.

Know That Tension Is Usually Temporary

Being in a minority means you stand out. Co-workers may rely on stereotypes and unconscious biases. At first other men might keep their distance or make comments that come across as insensitive. This can be hurtful and isolating. However, it is often a passing stage. As people get to know you, and understand that you are a reliable contributor, acceptance tends to follow. Guys often have this thing at work called the 'Circle of Trust'. You gain entry when they know they can be themselves around you, and not fear being reported to HR. But staying cool doesn't mean letting the guys cross the line – sexual harassment is never OK.

Women in minority can face far greater issues. If you believe it will help, take some time and explain your background or practices. Knowledge can help alleviate discrimination.

Deal With Discrimination But Avoid Being Too Easily Offended

As women, it is easier for us to recognise intolerance and discrimination because we face these issues regularly. It may be a subtle comment or a blatant outburst. First, differentiate between inadvertent insults and intentional ones. Consider letting go of unintentional slights.

Unfortunately, learning to withstand criticism is a necessity for women because whenever you choose to speak your mind, you are bound to offend someone. And when that happens, you are allowed to be upset but then move on realising that you can't really please everyone. Also, go back to Chapter 3 and re-read the strategies provided for understanding the context better for any negative limiting beliefs.

For the more serious and deliberate acts of prejudice, take control of your emotions first, then detach yourself from the situation and proceed to address it in the most effective way possible. Acknowledging that it's probably not about you doesn't mean you need to stay silent. Address the issue from a place of non-reactivity. By keeping it neutral and focusing on the desired future outcome, you express the intention to move things forward rather than wallowing in complaints.

If the situation isn't handled to your satisfaction, you can lodge a formal complaint with your Human Resources Department and/or consult a lawyer.

Avoid Injecting Gender In Every Discussion

Sometimes raising a concern itself is enough without playing the gender card. As sometimes, even the most well-intentioned bosses get irked by bringing this into discussions unless warranted and can get defensive. If in some situations your issue can not only be heard but addressed without specifically mentioning gender discrimination, then avoid it.

Don't Lose Your Identity

Just because you are in the minority, it doesn't mean losing your identity to 'fit in the crowd'. Don't be afraid to stand alone so you can be true to your heritage and/or values. Don't be afraid to do things your way. Believe in yourself and get your ideas out there. You don't have to round your edges to avoid appearing 'demanding' to someone else. Your edges give you strength and set you apart. Don't listen to anyone who tells you to fit into a pre-formed mould – go in, give it your all and make your mark in that field.

Leverage Your Uniqueness At Work

Turn your diversity into a competitive advantage and leverage your strengths. There are some gender-specific things that women are naturally good at. Whether it's listening, emotional aptitude, empathy, socialising or just being the den mother, if you have these strengths, play to them. They're good qualities to demonstrate as an emerging leader no matter where you work. Use this to become an exceptional leader who garners respect regardless of your gender.

A recent Stanford Business School study shows that women who can combine male and female qualities do better than everyone else, even men, where male qualities are defined as aggression, assertiveness and confidence. And the feminine qualities are defined as collaboration, process orientation, persuasion and humility.

The research followed 132 business school graduates for eight years and found that women who had so-called masculine traits but who tempered them with feminine traits were promoted 1.5 times faster.

Christine Lagarde, President of the International Monetary Fund, while speaking in an interview says: "Dare the difference. Make it your selling point. Don't try to measure yourself, your performance, your popularity against the standards and the yardsticks and the measurement men have used before you."

Make Decisions Quickly

Women, owing to their communal nature, tend to poll before decisions and take into account everyone's suggestion and feedback. Don't do that. In fact, if anything, make decisions quickly. It's hard to visualise someone as a leader if she is always waiting to be told what to do and feels the need to ask everyone's advice before arriving at any decision.

Know The Differences

Men and women have very different communication styles. I often found myself launching into long-winded explanations for projects when working with previous bosses, but over time I learned to adapt my communication style. Women are typically very verbose while men prefer brevity. Instead of rattling off a lengthy task list, I learned to focus my conversation by asking relevant questions that matter. Mentoring styles also differ between men and women. While women are eager to give and receive feedback and advice, men follow an experiential approach wherein they demonstrate via action. Keep that in mind.

Be Confident And Don't Be Afraid To Disagree

To stomach the male-dominated culture, women need to step into their power. People who carry themselves with confidence and speak their mind typically get noticed more. Go back to Chapter 2 and review some of the strategies you can deploy to appear more confident. Don't hesitate to disagree when it warrants. Remember, what is right should always be more important and bigger than your own ego. So, if you are wrong, then don't hesitate to admit it. In other words, disagree but don't be disagreeable. Sparking discussions can be heathy, but triggering disagreements without the use of tact can work against you.

Sheryl Sandberg recommends thinking personally, acting communally and combining niceness with insistence. Truth be told, I was quite offended when I first read this suggestion. Why do we have to cushion everything? Unfortunately, this is how it is. Women are expected to bring 'niceness' to the table. Sheryl notes that Mary Sue Coleman, President of University of Michigan calls this "relentlessly pleasant." Mary says: "This method involves smiling frequently, expressing appreciation and concern, invoking common interests emphasising larger goals and approaching the negotiation as solving a problem, as opposed to taking a critical stance." This method, though seeming compromising, yields better results than going after something, all out.

Despite everything, sometimes clients can still look past you, but don't let their hang-ups get to you. If you work hard and are determined, then eventually people will start seeing you above and beyond any barriers. Don't make your minority status your focus because if you do, chances are other people will do it too. Hold your head high at all times and know that it will always be your work that will speak for you as well as your will to succeed. It's this that will set you apart regardless of whether you are in a minority or not.

Don't Be Afraid To Ask for More

When it's time to ask for a promotion or pay rise, don't feel intimidated because you are different. Substantiate your case with evidence and do not hesitate to put yourself forward. Prepare your 'asks' in advance and furnish yourself with data that will back your case. Furthermore, convert your requests into statements.

Most bosses are too busy to figure out what the most equitable project allocation is. Those team members who can vocalise which opportunities and projects they prefer are always considered first. Your boss might be the type of leader who got to where he/she is by weighing up facts and figures, so equip yourself with information that demonstrates your strengths. The self-promotion techniques highlighted in the earlier chapter can add value here too.

Don't View Older Men In Authority As Father Figures

Many women have a tendency to do that and this makes the relationship difficult depending on the relationship you have had with your own father. Irrespective of the nature of relationship, putting men at work in the same category as fathers, grandfathers, brothers, husbands and sons can be detrimental for you as this changes the dynamics of professional relationships.

Join Affinity Networks

Take a look around your industry's community, online networks and social channels, and participate in company-sponsored affinity and networking groups. Join different women's business groups and meet-ups as they provide ongoing support, understanding and opportunities. You'll make great new friends too.

Bond And Network

The best career opportunities often come out of interactions outside the office. If you aren't invited to an event (this frequently happens to women), then create your own networking event and invite them instead. Look for events and opportunities where women and men can attend together. Building a network of the right people will help you move up the corporate social ladder. Try to mix and mingle by creating social interaction opportunities outside work hours as well, and this may very well include family gatherings.

Develop A Thick Skin And A Sense Of Humour

Humour is rarely discussed as an effective management tool. This is despite the fact that it "reduces hostility, deflects criticism, relieves tension, improves morale and helps communicate difficult messages," according to a *Harvard Business Review* article. That same article further notes that executives who use humour more often are more likely to be ranked as outstanding leaders. Of course, there's a difference between humour and harassment. Sometimes people say things so out of line that you should take it up with a supervisor or Human Resources manager. There's nothing funny about that. But in many other situations, humour helps to alleviate tension and grants us a graceful way to exit an uncomfortable situation.

Don't Be The Yes Woman

Research and several areas in the book already highlight how tough it is to climb the corporate ladder. Women have had to work harder and prove themselves much more as compared to their male colleagues. In such a situation it is easy to say yes to all projects just to be perceived as the 'good employee'. However, it's important to champion the projects that you value that are also in sync with your leadership's brand while refusing those that are not. Hence, stop volunteering for low-profile and low-impact assignments by refusing diplomatically but firmly.

Also, don't be afraid to take up new roles. Sometimes stability means diminished opportunity for growth, which can only be avoided by opening up to fresh and new projects.

Don't Be Anyone's Assistant If You Aren't One

If you're not someone's assistant, do not get into the habit of acting like one. Don't take notes, get coffee or make photocopies as you are only perpetuating the stereotype that it's a professional woman's role to nurture, serve and care. There may be exceptions but don't make it a regular thing. And if your male peers aren't contributing to the tasks then you shouldn't be doing it either. Develop boundaries of flexibility. If this is becoming a regular thing, you can say you want to pass the task and ask to rotate job duties.

Stay Visible By Promoting Yourself

Do not sit passively and wait to be noticed. Do not wait for opportunities to drop in your lap. Raise your visibility and showcase your knowledge in every way you can. Once you learn how to own your successes and flaunt your accomplishments, you will become more in demand, and your background becomes irrelevant.

Sheryl recommends not falling for the Tiara Syndrome: a terminology coined by Carol Frohlinger and Deborah Kolb, founders of Negotiating Women, and involves waiting for others to notice you and place a tiara on your head. In an ideal and perfect meritocracy that should be the case, but unfortunately that's not how it works. You need to make yourself visible and be willing to demand your own tiara.

Get A Sponsor / Mentor

During company reorganisations, mergers and massive layoffs, minorities are often twice as likely to be negatively impacted. Hence it is important to align yourself with the right people within your organisation and industry if you want to succeed. Identify sponsors who can promote you within your organisation. Hiring a mentor (male or female) could take you far. A mentor who has already seen the ups and downs of the industry will bode well for you when you are just starting out. A mentor also plays a huge role in introducing you to the challenges you will face and helps connect you with the right people that belong to his/her current network. However, many mentors don't do 'handholding', and don't assume that by connecting to a mentor you will automatically be pushed up a ladder and whisked away to a 'corner office'. Mentors will be most supportive when you are willing to take your own initiatives.

Coping Strategies To Succeed In Male-Dominated Industries

Understand That Not Everyone Will Open Up To You

Avoid Isolation And Communicate

Know That Tension Is Usually Temporary

Deal with Discrimination But Avoid Being Too Easily Offended

Avoid Injecting Gender In Every Discussion

Don't Lose Your Identity

Leverage Your Uniqueness at Work

Make Decisions Quickly

Know The Differences

Be Confident And Don't Be Afraid To Disagree

Don't Be Afraid To Ask for More

Don't View Older Men In Authority As Father Figures

Join Affinity Networks

Bond And Network

Develop A Thick Skin And A Sense of Humour

Don't Be The Yes Woman

Don't Be Anyone's Assistant If You Aren't One

Stay Visible By Promoting Yourself

Get A Sponsor / Mentor

CHAPTER 10:

WORKPLACE HARASSMENT

The world is making strides in women's empowerment and advancement and women are also making progress in the workplace. But then we saw the recent #metoo campaign and thousands of cases emerge where women have been subject to various forms of harassment. The media has also exposed several other high-profile cases involving top-notch celebrities. All of these incidents put a spotlight on an issue that still remains an all too frequent reality in the workplace: sexual harassment. Sexual harassment is a deep-rooted problem that has nothing to do with class or culture. Alarming statistics indicate it is an epidemic that is prevalent across the globe.

I honestly believe there are only a handful of women in the entire world who have never experienced some form of harassment, be it explicit or implicit. Unfortunately, some women experience far worse scenarios than others. Whether it's an inappropriate touch or nudge in a public place where men seem to conveniently and deliberately brush past you… whether it's an indecent or awkward stare… whether it's an improper comment or conversation that makes you uncomfortable… *we all* have been there one way or another.

Women around the world, from developing countries and established communities, are so used to staying quiet when being subject to any form of harassment. The term harassment itself is used so loosely that unless it's physical harassment, most people think that everything else outside of that category is acceptable. Many women choose to stay quiet in much worse situations. They have been dismissing inappropriate advances as 'normal' for a long time, but that doesn't mean they should continue ignoring them forever.

I recently mentored some young girls who had just begun their career. Whilst casually discussing challenges at work, one of the girls expressed her discomfort with a senior male colleague who repeatedly addressed her at work as 'sweetheart' and 'darling'. He would also pat her shoulder every now and then. Her experience was disturbing, but it was even more appalling how she dismissed her own concern and undermined its seriousness: "I know I am overreacting and being silly and childish. He is my father's age and it probably doesn't mean much. But I am not a kid anymore. Anyway, I am not the only one he does this to. He does that to everyone."

The rest of the girls nodded in agreement and laughed it off as well. I was speechless. Not only did this girl believe, or was made to believe, that inappropriate names were actually acceptable, she was also finding excuses to defend her manager's harassing behaviour. That's when it struck me that perhaps one of the primary reasons sexual harassment goes unchecked is because the abuser makes the victim believe that his harassing behaviour is OK. Inappropriate actions under the guise of 'It's my nature', 'It's not just you', 'I did it once only', or it was 'just a compliment' are some of the common excuses serial sexual harassers use to justify their sick behaviour.

Another concern is that every time a woman raises a harassment issue, she faces more criticism than the harasser himself. No educated woman in her right frame of mind will lash out at anyone publicly unless the offender hits a nerve. Unfortunately, women who choose to raise their voice are doubted, accused of seeking attention and ridiculed for waiting so long to publicise the issue. Often we are setting a bad example by holding the victim more accountable than the offender, and thereby discouraging women even more.

Age and seniority have nothing to do with this issue. I recently heard that a very senior manager was fired from my ex-company on account of sexual harassment. My colleagues and I were shocked. Not only was he one of the most respected managers at the company, some of us fondly called him 'granddad'! Apparently, he had been portraying a very different image to us while he behaved inappropriately with new recruits in other departments. That experience taught me an important lesson: just because someone looks mature and respectful doesn't mean they are acting appropriately. These incidents prompted me to write many blogs around this topic that some still consider taboo. By bringing attention to this issue, I am working to empower female victims and re-establish appropriate behaviour in the workplace.

You see, it's not just the harassers that we need to stop. We as women need to make ourselves strong enough to be able to raise a voice and unleash a backlash on such offenders while teaching them a lesson or two.

Social media is more powerful than it ever was. In Susan Fowler's case, the media pounced on the offenders with extreme vitriol. The #deleteuber campaign reached new heights, and the Harvey Weinstein scandal, amongst many others, proved that media has the power to highlight social injustices and evoke remedial measures like never before. We need to make use of every medium out there to make our voice heard.

In many work scenarios, it may not be sexual harassment per se, but misogynist mindsets create gender-based biases. Publicly trashing ideas with the intention to belittle others, scoffing and dismissing suggestions in meetings, making assumptions about career choices, taking ill-informed decisions regarding career paths, openly making snide remarks and frequently denouncing female team members at work – these are some of the common characteristics of workplace misogynists and bullies.

American bullying experts Drs Gary and Ruth Namie define bullying as a "repeated, health-harming mistreatment of a person by one or more workers that takes the form of verbal abuse; conduct or behaviors that are threatening, intimidating, or humiliating; sabotage that prevents work from getting done; or some combination of the three."

The bully aims to assault the dignity, trustworthiness, competence and self-worth of the target to derive personal gains or sadistic satisfaction that often leaves the target feeling responsible, guilty, isolated and confused.

If you are a victim of sexual harassment or bullying, here is what you need to know and do:

Identify The Behaviour And Call It Out

The very first thing you need to do if you believe you are a victim is to identify what is happening. If any behaviour repeatedly makes you feel uncomfortable, then you are probably not overreacting. The first step towards countering harassment is to realise that it's happening. Once you say what it is, you are opening yourself to different possibilities of handling it.

Harassment can be physical, verbal and/or non-verbal, can happen to anyone in any environment, and it can be either a 'one-off' or series of incidents. A key test, though, is how the behaviour makes the victim feel. The European Community Code of Practice describes it as 'unwanted or unwelcome conduct of a sexual nature, or other conduct based on sex, affecting the dignity of women and men at work'. This can include unwelcome physical, verbal or non-verbal conduct.

According to Louisa Symington-Mills, *The Telegraph's* career agony aunt: "No one should have to endure such behaviour in the workplace – or anywhere else. Behaviour that is unwelcome and intimidating can transform an office environment from harmonious to odious, and may have immediate implications on the health and happiness of the recipient, as well as the wellbeing of those that work closely with them. Determining whether or not a comment or action directed towards you is inappropriate is often subjective, but if you feel upset and uncomfortable as a result, then it's very likely to be, and may even be, harassment."

There are two types of sexual harassment: 1. **Quid Pro Quo** – the Latin phrase that means 'this for that'. In essence, this type of harassment occurs when an employer says that they will give an employee this job, this promotion, or this benefit, for that sexual favour; 2. **Hostile Environment** – this type of harassment is much more difficult to pin down. It occurs when the harassing behaviour creates a hostile, negative work environment for the employee.

Many harassers use several types of excuses to vindicate themselves such as:

1. *"She laughed at my joke so I thought she didn't mind."* Some employees feel obligated to participate or laugh for fear of being negatively judged. Just because they smiled doesn't mean they are not uncomfortable.

2. *"It happened on a business trip, so it doesn't count."* Whether it took place in an office environment or outside of it, it doesn't change the context. It's still harassment.

3. *"It was just a compliment."* Compliments that make the other person uneasy fall under harassment too.

4. *"It only happened once."* It's still harassment, whether it happened once or 20 times.

5. *"The comments were directed at someone else."* If you witness inappropriate comments (such as your colleague commenting on how someone else might be in bed, without that person present), you can still file a sexual harassment complaint.

6. *"Sexual harassment is all about sex, and sex didn't happen."* Inappropriate touching and verbal harassment, whether direct or indirect, is still harassment.

7. *"This is the way I've grown up; you can't expect me to change."* Other people at your workplace are not expected to adjust to your behaviour just because you alone think it's socially acceptable.

The US Merit Systems Protection Board recognises that unwelcome behaviour can fall into seven categories: sexual teasing, remarks, jokes, or questions; pressure for dates; letters, email, telephone calls, or materials of a sexual nature; sexual looks or gestures; deliberate touching, leaning over, cornering, or pinching; pressure for sexual favours; actual/attempted sexual assault or rape. Sometimes it may include giving gifts of a personal nature. My father highlighted a very important difference between personal and non-personal gifts at the beginning of my career which I found to be a very useful benchmark for accepting gifts from male colleagues. Personal gifts include all such gifts that come in contact with your body, such as cosmetics, perfume, clothes, accessories etc, and are often unacceptable to many women. Non-personal gifts include books, mugs, stationery items and decoration pieces and can be acceptable. Whereas this situation may be more a personal choice, the purpose is to know the difference.

Other behaviours include asking sexual questions, such as questions about someone's sexual history or their sexual orientation.

Know That It's Not Your Fault And You Are Not Alone

If you are being harassed, realise that it's not your fault, and it has nothing to do with your actions or who you are as a person. Take control of your emotions and detach yourself from the abuse. You did not incur this on yourself, nor do you deserve it. You are also not alone. New Trades Union Congress (TUC) research indicates that more than half of the women surveyed say they have been sexually harassed at work and most admit to not reporting it. In their survey of 1,500 people, one of the key findings revealed that *"More than half (52%) of all women polled have experienced some form of sexual harassment."*

In the vast majority of cases, the perpetrator was a male colleague, with nearly one in five reporting that their direct manager or someone else with direct authority over them was the perpetrator.

TUC head Frances O'Grady said it left women feeling ashamed and frightened. Many of those who told their stories also said they felt unable to report what had happened to them because they were embarrassed or feared losing their job. Another Slater & Gordon survey found that six in ten working women believed a male colleague had behaved inappropriately towards them, whilst more than a third reported a senior male colleague had made inappropriate comments about their body or the clothes they were wearing.

Ignoring The Abuser Will Do You More Harm Than Good

When harassing behaviour remains unchecked, the harasser repeats that behaviour, each time more audacious than before. Unfortunately, the moment you decide to ignore or let go of a harasser there is no looking back. Ignoring or avoiding the abuser may seem like the safest way to proceed, but it's actually more harmful; the victim suffers in silence and the problem doesn't get resolved. Trying to appease the abuser or complying with him is not a solution either. Bullying or harassment is a power struggle. Once you give into one demand, they will push for more.

Start Issuing Warnings

According to a training released by Velsoft on sexual harassment, you should start with a verbal notice and tell the harasser what they are doing is not acceptable in a calm, unemotional tone of voice. In my *HuffPost* article on dealing with bullies, I suggest that "if they are invading your comfort zone in terms of physical space, place a physical boundary (like a desk) between you and them, or ask them to step back. If emotional space is being threatened, such as asking personal questions or offering unwarranted advice, tell them to stop, politely yet firmly."

A statement like "Get your hands off," is firm, assertive rather than aggressive, and non-negotiable. You should also start keeping a written record of events, times, dates, and people who witnessed the events. Even if the issue is resolved after this first step, you need to document what happened. If the harasser continues his/her behaviour, repeat the first step but make it stronger. Something like: "I have already told you to stop touching me. If you don't stop, I will report you for harassment" repeats the original message, and is still assertive and non-negotiable. Make sure you keep your tone of voice calm and unemotional but be assertive as this will be crucial in deterring the harassers.

Start issuing written warnings and keep a record. Write the person an email or letter and send it to them. This letter should share the same tone as the other warnings: firm, assertive, and non-negotiable. It should restate the points you made in your verbal warnings. Make sure you do not threaten the harasser; stay as unemotional as possible. Also make sure you keep a copy of these letters for your records.

Make An Informal Harassment Inquiry

If you are unable to deter your harasser, or if you believe there is serious risk in confronting your harasser (such as being physically harmed or losing your job), Velsoft next recommends going to your manager, your company's Human Resources department, or the company's harassment officer. They will typically give you their opinion about the claim: whether it is more or less serious than the complainant perceives and what options he/she has next. Be aware that this step may place your complaint on record. No matter what the outcome of this meeting, be sure to record its details and add it to your log of events.

Make A Formal Complaint In The Organisation

This step turns the complaint into a formal process. Both parties (the complainant and the alleged harasser) have a lot at stake here: their reputation, their job, and possibly their career. According to Velsoft, if you have events documented and recorded, you will feel a lot more secure in raising a formal complaint. However, be aware that this step will probably bring the issue to the attention of your co-workers. Investigators usually try to maintain your privacy as much as possible, but they will likely need to talk to your co-workers to confirm events. The process of raising a complaint is not always a bitter and prolonged one. Sometimes the harasser and the complainant can meet to discuss the incident(s) and come out with a better understanding of each other and what happened. If your harassment issue has not been resolved by the first four steps, this will be the last opportunity to resolve it in-house.

Make A Formal Complaint With The Government

In most countries, there is an agency that governs against harassment and discrimination. You should consult a lawyer before filing a complaint with this organisation or agency. Some areas have time limits. The EEOC in the United States, for example, requires filing no later than 180 to 300 days after the alleged incident, depending on the state where you live.

I do realise that the above steps may be helpful on paper but difficult in execution. What's more, many organisations, particularly the HR departments, may not be supportive. Sometimes HR departments only work to serve the company's interest and are hence not very keen on any harassment claims that can lead to suing the company. Hence, often as a victim, you would need to channel your own inner strength and report the incident. Then leverage your network and start your job search. Once you find a new job, use tweets, reviews and blogs, whatever you can, to share your story. A lawyer in Pakistan recently shared a screen shot of harassing comments she was receiving from her male colleague. She also shared this man's social media. Within hours that post was storming the social media and everyone knew who that man was. Needless to say, he never dared to repeat the offence!

You can also start your own affinity or staff network group, which can help you unionise without unionising. These groups serve to look after the interests and concerns of their members.

Life is often hard and unfair. You need to learn to fight your own battles. Don't always depend on other people to come to your rescue. You need to be your own saviour. Nothing is more important than your self-respect and integrity and only you can make everyone else realise that too. It's never too late to stand up and fight your own battle. As they say, "The best time to start was yesterday, the next best time is now," and once you have stood up and fought your own battle successfully, come forward and help others fight theirs.

Coping Strategies To Address Workplace Harassment

Identify The Behaviour And Call It Out

Know That It's Not Your Fault And You Are Not Alone

Ignoring The Abuser Will Do You More Harm Than Good

Start Issuing Warnings

Make An Informal Harassment Inquiry

Make A Formal Complaint In The Organisation

Make A Formal Complaint With The Government

CHAPTER 11:

LACK OF INFRASTRUCTURE AND SUPPORT

I have already highlighted how even when playing the same game, men and women are subject to different standards. But perhaps one of the biggest challenges women face on their way to the top is that we work and live in a world, culture and system that is designed for men. Without the proper infrastructure, women are unable to achieve unfettered career success. This is prevalent all over the world. In the absence of a work environment that prioritises protecting women from harassment, bullying and sexism, where laws, rules and systems are more favourable for men than they are for women, there is little surprise as to why a large majority of women find it very challenging to make it to the top.

The very tenor of most work environments underscores a dichotomy of opportunities and ensuing success between men and women. There is dire need to build on-ramps to the highway of economic opportunity for women. Just as a rising tide lifts all boats, a virtuous cycle that encourages women to participate in our economy will in turn present them as leaders in their families, communities and neighbourhoods.

Even though women today are more empowered, confident and bold than they ever were, this didn't happen overnight; it's been a long list of advocates for women's rights throughout history that is responsible for where we are today. These champions have fought long and hard for equality, and they continue the fight today. And that fight is far from being over, even after 100 years of suffrage.

Writer, broadcaster and award-winning activist, Caroline Criado Perez, is one such powerful feminist who has been actively campaigning for women's rights. Perez has made many significant contributions to our cause and has support from high-profile women like Emma Watson and JK Rowling. Perez is responsible for placing the statue of suffragist Millicent Fawcett in Parliament Square. This important symbol of women's rights depicts Fawcett standing her ground in a group of men. Among her many other achievements, Caroline has also ensured women are represented on UK banknotes – that's why we now have UK £10 notes featuring Jane Austen.

Recently, I had the honour of not only meeting this amazing lady but also canvassing with her to support the Women's Equality Party. Meeting Caroline filled me with hope. Just like statues and currency notes, we are capable of achieving so much more when we fight for what we believe in.

I know it seems like a far-fetched idea and that we have a long way to go, but there is always a first time for everything. Women have enormous power. We are voters. We are consumers. Did you know that women make a large percentage of every country's consumer decisions? And with this power, we can exert real pressure to push for a change in course for those issues we care about.

The culture and system keeps the role of a career professional and mother mutually exclusive when in reality it's not. Yes, personal choices are often influenced by social binds, peer pressure and familial expectations. But most career women who have cited powerful reasons to opt out can be retained if only the infrastructure (inclusive policies) was more favourable.

A woman's role as the primary care giver for her children is not just a cultural expectation, but as Caroline says: "It's also built into our laws. The US Census Bureau considers the mother to be the designated parent, even if both parents are present in the home. When it's a mother caring for her children it's called parenting, and when a father takes care of children it's called child arrangement. UK public policy also reinforces that the mother is a child's primary carer. Child benefits are paid to mothers while men still use the term 'babysitting' to look after their own children. Women try their best to overcome these challenges, but as someone rightly noted: 'The world has a way of reminding women that they are women and the girls that they are girls'."

However, there are steps that you can take to address the infrastructure gap. Here they go:

Champion A Pro-Women System In Your Organisations

Getting the women to the top will require effort from all sides. It takes two to tango. Once we have mastered our internal challenges, organisations need to deploy systems and policies to facilitate us in navigating a system designed for men. And for that we will need to raise our concerns and ensure they are being addressed. You can play an important role in this by joining staff networks and affinity groups that can push for such changes.

Sometimes, all it takes is creating awareness. It's important to realise that we cannot change what we are not aware of. Talking about the challenges and creating awareness can transform minds and this can be achieved through active campaigning. As *Girl Boss* author Sophia says: "You will do it not by whining but by fighting. You don't get taken seriously by asking someone to take you seriously. You have got to show up and own it."

There are several areas where women are at a disadvantage. Take, for example, gender data. In the special feminist edition of the *New European*, Caroline Criado Perez recognises how important it is among other things to close the gender data gap. "There is a frightening amount we don't know about women. From medical research to car safety to economic statistics, the vast majority of the world's data is based on men – male bodies and male lives. The result is that medication is less likely to work for women and is more likely to cause (more severe) adverse reactions." If you work for an organisation that is responsible for such data, you can press for data parity.

The organisation policies need to reflect gender parity too. From recruitment to talent management, appraisal to compensation, management needs to revisit all policies and systems for their organisation to check for overt and covert bias. Staff members need training on conscious and unconscious bias, and every decision needs to be informed by a structured due diligence process. Corporate leaders need to hold their managers accountable for diversity decisions while discouraging any and all stereotypes that influence those decisions.

HR professionals should identify rising female talent throughout the organisation and track their career paths and accomplishments. What's more, a company should implement steps to develop this female talent: they need access to informal networks, influential mentors and stretch assignments (eg in a line role). Soliciting feedback is a critical part of this development process so that management can identify and address any subtle filters. Your affinity group can work with an organisation's HR department to effect these changes quickly and wherever possible.

Recently, Rebecca Johnson's tweet made the rounds on social media. She tweeted a picture of her child with this caption: 'At a massive professional conference. Brought the baby. People seem astounded. Here's the thing: if you want women in positions of authority, you have to get comfortable with motherhood. You're welcome."

The tweet quickly went viral, resulting in 10,000 retweets, thousands of likes and more than 850 comments from followers. Some were in support of Johnson's point while others strongly objected. This is not the first time the issue has been debated in the public forum. Italian MEP Licia Ronzulli has been in the press numerous times for taking her young daughter into Parliament, while earlier Australian Senator Larissa Waters made international headlines for breastfeeding her two-month-old daughter during a parliamentary vote.

I for one am always delighted to read such news as I am one of those mums who often takes her seven-year-old to events, whenever she can. Initially, I was new and hesitant to rely on any unknown care givers, but even when I did find a trusted care giver, I began to realise that hiring help is expensive and thus a luxury. My husband is a pretty hands-on dad, but ever since we moved, his workload has been enormous. Nevertheless, he was quick to volunteer when I had commitments outside of school hours. But then again, there were emergency situations where he was often held back at work at a moment's notice. What would I do then? Leave the event? No way. I always ask permission to bring my son along. Since he is much older now and an avid reader, he brings a book and accompanies me when I travel to events. Occasionally, he even interacts with conference guests.

Some event managers gave permission willingly, while others were more reluctant and only agreed because they didn't have a choice. Some clearly said no, but that was all right too as some events are designed that way. At the conference itself, I received a range of reactions to having my son in tow. Some women looked at me with sympathy. Some said they were proud of me, some rolled their eyes, and some just ignored me. Soon I learned to disregard judgmental looks and rolling eyes. If it was working for us and the organisers didn't have an issue, then why should I care what people think, especially since I would likely never meet them again! I stopped being cautious.

Sometimes I wish that events had a disclaimer, just like some restaurants do: pets are welcome here. How nice would it be to see signs at events and workplaces that say: *Children and pets are welcome here!* Should we start a movement?

Women should be offered flexi-time, job-sharing opportunities and work from home options as much as possible. Men should also have access to similar choices. An employee physically working within an office doesn't necessarily guarantee improved results or productivity. Flexible work hours, work from home opportunities, job sharing, and part-time jobs (when appropriate), are options that organisations can evaluate to ensure they retain talented mothers during their child-rearing years.

Organisations should additionally try to incorporate on-site childcare facilities wherever possible. This might not be easy to implement, but many companies have successfully done so already. Moreover, studies indicate that employee performance is higher and absenteeism lower among employees using on-site versus off-site childcare. On-site crèche facilities offer convenience and peace of mind. The employees feel valued and work harder to exceed expectations. In addition, on-site childcare also helps reduce tardiness and stress while alleviating separation anxiety. Plus, children in the workplace can add much-needed energy and cheer and help employees be more mindful of aggressive, disruptive conflicts.

In the Eastern culture, there is not much concept of parental leave for the fathers. Even in the developed countries, statistics evidence that men do not fully take advantage of this leave. And organisations don't push either. By encouraging fathers to take full advantage of parenting leave, some of the responsibilities that have been undertaken by women single-handedly for so long can be divided.

Even if you are not part of decision- or policy-making in your organisation, you can still play a significant role in outlining an agenda which champions the aforementioned policy recommendations.

Advocate For Pro-Women Laws

"If you want to build a more equal country, you need to push equality for women into the political space," says Sophie Walker, leader of the Women's Equality Party. And this essentially means supporting political parties that put women's equality at the top of their agenda. Though I have never been very active in politics, this party's manifesto really resonates with me and I have been actively campaigning with them for the same reasons.

Over the last 100 years, we have witnessed the introduction of many progressive laws that support gender equality. Women can now own property on the same terms as men, serve on a jury, open a bank account and apply for a loan. Today we can sit in the House of Lords, work on the London Stock Exchange, secure a court order against an abusive spouse, get a legal abortion and report marital rape. If these became possible, other laws can too!

Some laws even after they have been passed need our attention. The Equal Pay Act is one of them. Even though it was enacted in 1983, equal pay is still an issue; women lose out on nearly £140 billion a year given the gender pay gap. Recent pay gap reports indicate that women are also paid less than half of the salaries paid to men working for some of the UK's biggest companies.

Free universal childcare is necessary to benefit both women and the economy. In 2015, McKinsey estimated that global GDP would grow by $12 trillion were women able to engage in the paid labour force at the same rate as men. But they aren't. Caroline Criado Perez, the powerful activist mentioned earlier, highlights that: "The Women's Budget Group has calculated that investing 2% of GDP in the caring industries would generate up to 1.5 million jobs in the UK, compared to 750,000 for an equivalent investment in construction. That cash infusion would create almost as many jobs for men, and up to four times as many for women – and the investment required is much smaller than the annual tax giveaways introduced in 2010 that have disproportionately benefited men.

Research supports that investing in universal childcare reduces education spend overall (as less remedial education is needed), and increases the productivity of future generations. There is simply no argument against doing this, and doing it now."

In my recent podcast interview with inspiring rape survivor Madeleine Black, we discussed how shocking it is to see many violent criminals and rapists walk free after serving lenient sentences for their crimes. Britain has the lowest rape conviction rate in Europe. Furthermore, there is no proper support system to help or counsel victims.

We need to pass additional laws that protect victims' rights and make women feel safe and equal. Some laws are downright ridiculous and need to be overturned. For example, an employer can still legally require female employees to wear high heels because the government rejected a law that would have banned this type of sexist behaviour in the workplace. Men, on the other hand, must dress with an 'equivalent level of smartness'. Law against banning 'upskirting' was recently blocked by an MP. However, with powerful rallying, hopes are high that this bill will be passed soon and the gap in the law closed.

In my native country of Pakistan, The Corporate Governance Code implemented under the Companies Act of 2017 requires all public interest companies (those listed on the stock exchange and others with or above a specified threshold of paid-up capital, turnover, employees and shareholders), to hire at least one female director. Given Pakistan ranks low in gender equality issues, this is indeed a remarkable step that compels organisations to do the needful.

Pro-women laws ensure future economies will be dynamic and inclusive – offering equal opportunity to everyone. And even if you are not in the government, you can still lobby for such laws, write letters and sign petitions just as Caroline does. Even little actions count and can potentially make a huge difference. Your one step forward could possibly inspire several others to do the same. However, creating meaningful laws is as important as enforcing them otherwise the battle for women's rights is only half won.

Support Non-Profit Organisations Working For Women

There is a plethora of organisations working tirelessly to defend women's rights. Many women have fought to secure what we enjoy today as basic rights. In many parts of the world, women are still abused, traded, mutilated and deprived of education. Honour killings, child brides, and acid attacks remain a sad reality for hundreds of women worldwide. These women need our support! Recent women's marches across the globe highlight what we are capable of when we organise and mobilise. When you are part of an organisation working to support women, you have a proper platform to champion issues important to you and connect with like-minded individuals.

Elicit Support From Men

"Gender equality is your issue too," said actor and UN Women's Goodwill Ambassador, Emma Watson, when addressing men in one of her recent speeches. #HeForShe was launched by the United Nations in September 2014 as a movement that aims to inspire and encourage men to take action against gender inequality. Men are often oblivious to the challenges women face in their career. According to Professor Paul Boyle, Vice Chancellor, University of Leicester, men don't think gender equality is their concern or is a critical issue that warrants change. As he notes: "In our institutions, gender equality discussions are dominated by women while men are getting on with research and other activities."

To truly advocate women's equality, do not dismiss the value that men can provide; encourage them to step up and play their part. It's not them versus us.

Raise Your Voice And Call Out Inequality

Highlight issues surrounding inequality wherever you can and help people understand it better by writing blogs, sharing articles, or perhaps by doing live videos with meaningful messages; even tweeting hashtags of popular movements that support the theme is a perfectly acceptable way to show your support. But don't just stop at that. Social media is a very important tool with an impact far more outreaching than we can ever imagine, and what's more, it's free! Challenge and counteract media that intentionally or unintentionally undermine women rights, make sure your voice is being heard by raising your concerns and registering your complaints where appropriate.

To appreciate the power of social media, I highly recommend reading the book *Saving Bletchley Park* written by my latest inspiration Dr Sue Black. A single mum of three, Dr Black started off as a woman refugee. Today, Black is close to tech royalty, having almost single-handedly saved Bletchley Park, centre of Britain's World War II code-breaking efforts, from imminent closure in the early 2000s through the sheer power of social media.

Even small acts of resistance can make a difference. According to Samantha Rennie, Executive Director at Rosa: "People must be held accountable for their thoughts and their actions, so when you see acts of sexism, racism, xenophobia, ableism, Islamophobia or anything else, call it out!" Sometimes people do not realise what's wrong until someone points it out, so don't hesitate to point out and raise awareness in suitable ways.

Recently my seven-year-old son pointed out when I was explaining to him the concepts of gender equality and the gender pay gap that his favourite book series had fewer books for girls than they had for boys. He said to me: "Mama, now I know what you mean when you say girls have been getting less. They should make more girl books!" I must confess that I hadn't noticed that before!

I was amazed and actually pleased that he noticed something which I have been missing or would ordinarily miss. He was also quick to justify the author and said that though there should be more girl books, the author didn't mean to. He made the boy books first and probably ran out of ideas and that's why the girl series has fewer numbers. This also made me realise that children have such a pure and malice-free thought process. Not once did he want to attribute the fewer numbers to 'women are less than equal' notion. So all the 'social conditioning' that comes later is what we pass on to them and what they absorb from the society biases.

I was reading about Caroline Perez in an article, and the way the author described her stood out to me. What the author wrote really opened my eyes and can perhaps explain why I was pleased when my son pointed out the difference in numbers. Here is what it says: "Criado Perez has a genius for seeing things that the rest of us miss, and for bringing invisible women out of the shadows, directing our attention to history's forgotten narratives. She has an unerring, unnerving sense of social and cultural blind spots and recognises absence, the space between the lines. For decades, for instance, I've seen these bronze statesmen in Parliament Square but not really seen them, just as I handled banknotes without really noticing what was on them (the faces of white men). We live in a world in which men are the default humans; we don't realise women aren't there because they've always been not-there, and we've never known anything different."

Support Other Women

Back in the old days, unfortunately, many young women including myself grew up in working culture strife with gas lighting and queen bees. Wikipedia describes 'queen bee' as someone who sees other, usually younger, women as competitors and will refuse to help them advance within a company, preferring to mentor a male over a female employee.

An Ellevate Network poll revealed that more than half the respondents had been 'queen bee'd'. A 2010 survey by the Workplace Bullying Institute reported that female bullies directed their hostilities towards other women 80% of the time – up 9% since 2007. And a 2011 study by the American Management Association found that 95% of working women believed they were undermined by another woman at some point in their careers.

Another trend which is predominant amongst several women is the lack of tolerance and openness towards an opposing viewpoint. There is absolutely no need to bring down another woman and pass belittling or condescending comments about her choices just to prove your point and satisfy your ego. Be vocal and express your viewpoint by all means, but within the limits of propriety and without sounding derogatory. Also remember that each woman has her own right to choose whatever is best suited to her. Definition of success has many layers. Just because someone doesn't share your passion of reaching the top at the same pace as you doesn't make her any less ambitious. For these women, quality of life may be more important than making it to the top, and that's OK. To each her own.

Pursuing a high-flying career does not give you licence to wrinkle your nose at stay-at-home mums either. A woman could be a stay-at-home mum or not a mum at all. Similarly, if you choose to take that career break it doesn't mean you start labelling career women who don't. The whole point of feminism and being in it together for me is to embrace choices and to let every other woman be free to do whatever she pleases, and look however she desires.

Susan Dench, founder and CEO of Success & Co, highlights the 'Woman Scorned Theory', which she believes is common as women tend to have long memories and take things personally when it comes to being slighted or criticised. However, the good news is that the 'queen bee' culture is gradually dissipating, and women are increasingly thinking of other women as allies, nurturing relationships, celebrating their unique strengths and making powerful collaborations. Supporting each other and lifting each other up is and will be our key to our success if we wish to get to the top.

Maria Shriver says this: "For so long women have been divided. Women who are mothers versus women who are not, women who work at home versus women who work outside the home, those who are married versus those who aren't, pro-life women versus pro-choice, white women versus women of colour, Democrat versus Republican, gay versus straight, and young versus old. It feels like the last issue where women came together was fighting for the right to vote. It's time to come together again."

Mentor Boys And Girls And Raise Their Aspirations

And we have already read enough of what social conditioning does to us. The harm has already been done to our generation and the ones before us, and perhaps that's why we write such books. But it's not too late to raise the aspirations of the existing generation and make them think differently.

These days, a lot is being said about the importance of female role models. Girls often look to the women in their lives for guidance and inspiration. How we act and what we do can set positive examples for girls to follow. In my article *Dear Girls, We Have Your Back* published on Ellevate, I discuss how important it is to support and empower young girls these days and why it's crucial to have female mentors for female students. After all, when you empower girls, they say, you are raising the quality of life for everyone. It is these very girls that will lead children by example, lead businesses, lead communities and even lead the country one day, and by mentoring and raising their aspirations we are laying the ground for a future generation of women who have the power to create a difference.

We are already facing a long list of challenges owing to social conditioning, but let's change that by teaching both our boys and girls to be responsible, empowered and empathetic individuals.

Teach your girls to be as brave as your boys. Teach them to step up, own success and give themselves permission to fail or to be imperfect. Teach your boys to be brave enough to point out injustice, inequality and intolerant behaviour. Teach them both the concepts of equal and shared parenting.

Teach girls to be kind, not nice. Niceness won't keep them safe. Kindness can and should be taught. Niceness, however, springs from a desire to please others, even if it's at our own expense. "For the most part, 'nice' means: be tolerant and accommodating," writes Shefali Tsabary, a clinical psychologist and author of *The Awakened Family*. "If we are brutally honest with ourselves, it also implies: do whatever it takes to keep the peace." Instead of teaching our girls to be nice, argues Tsabary, we should teach them how to be themselves, to be self-aware, "which means self-directed, self-governed, true to themselves."

You are now needed more than ever to be a role model for both girls and boys to look up to. But remember, they say that to be a role model is a privilege. Exercise that privilege wisely.

Strategies For A Better Infrastructure

Champion A Pro-Women System In Your Organisations

Advocate For Pro-Women Laws

Support Non-Profit Organisations Working For Women

Elicit Support From Men

Raise Your Voice And Call Out Inequality

Support Other Women

Mentor Boys And Girls And Raise Their Aspirations

CLOSING REMARKS

At this point, you are well versed in the range of challenges professional women just like you face on a daily basis. What's more, you now have a range of strategies you can employ to cope with, and ultimately overcome, those challenges effectively. Figure out which strategies resonate best with you at work, then integrate those solutions throughout your personal life too.

You may want to hire support like an external coach or an accountability partner to help you through the process for the first time. Remember, ultimately you are your own best rescuer so don't wait to be saved – save yourself!

To that point, the foundation of these strategies lies in a positive attitude about yourself. Self-acceptance is critical if you want to achieve your career goals. An inability to accept, self-validate and love yourself – right now, as you are, with all your flaws and foibles intact – condemns you to an endless cycle of dissatisfaction. No amount of external validation will ever be enough if you cannot first accept and love yourself. The best kind of confidence is derived from internal self-worth as anything dependent on others can be shaky.

Yes, workplace biases, harassment and lack of infrastructure are significant detriments to confidence and progress. A slump in your confidence is natural. But that's when you step back, revisit the challenges noted in this book and answer sincerely. Are external challenges an impediment to your growth or are internal challenges more of an issue? Or is it a combination of both? If there is even a slight chance that you can improve your situation by mastering your internal obstacles, then don't linger on anything else for long. Work on improving yourself first.

Bear in mind that the way to the top is never easy. There are many bumps and detours on your journey that will discourage you, but dig deep and be resilient. Trust yourself to get there. Navigating this path requires patience, determination and motivation. Setbacks are inevitable, but understanding them as learning experiences rather than failures will help you maintain positive momentum.

Congratulations to you, if you have already climbed the corporate ladder into a leadership position or made significant strides towards accomplishing your career goals. You should be as proud of yourself as I am of you! I know you are making many compromises to pursue your career, especially if you are a working mother. Be proud of your choices. Your grit and determination is admirable.

It's important to share what you've learned with other women who can benefit from your guidance; remember, we are all in this together.

I know you are compassionate to others but least forgiving of yourself. Aim high but appreciate you are only human. Self-compassion is that safety net that enables you to try more. It motivates you because it's what cushions your failure. Do not paralyse yourself with self-loathing. Your internal self-evaluation can sometimes be fastidious, but afford yourself the same leverage you afford others.

Give yourself permission to not know everything...

Give yourself permission to fail...

Give yourself permission to make mistakes...

Give yourself permission to let go...

Give yourself permission to miss out, and not have everything at the same time...

Give yourself permission to delegate or outsource...

Give yourself permission to hit the pause button and take time out for yourself...

Give yourself permission to self-promote...

Give yourself permission to be vulnerable...

You owe this to yourself!

I know you often compare, but defining yourself through other people's achievements is chasing the fool's paradise. I recently received an award at a ceremony where the theme was 'I made it' and there I heard the best advice I have heard in ages while I sat there pondering whether I had actually 'made it' or not. It was then I heard these powerful words from one of the speakers: "You make it to your own level, not to other people's level." Keep those words in mind.

I know you have the skills. It's just self-belief that you lack, but don't let doubt consume you. Yes, there are certain traits that are fixed and hard to influence. But the good news is that most soft skills such as confidence and self-belief are malleable and can be acquired. Practise them again and again until they become the norm.

I know you are susceptible to seize any chance to think badly of yourself. Just a little nudge asking you how sure you are about something rattles your confidence and makes you have a much skewed perception of your abilities and work. But trim those debilitating feelings and behaviours to size using all the strategies given. And then recalibrate your confidence compass by building firewalls that keep toxic thoughts in check.

I know you want to avoid risk when you fear a dig in approval and/or you fear losing. But remember you can't always win and you can't always be lucky. Don't berate yourself when you fail. Pick yourself up, wipe your tears and continue to fight on, and when you get up again know that there will be performance jitters. But perform anyway. If you did it once, you can do it again. Remember to acknowledge your role when you win. Don't sideline your performance.

I know sometimes you take things too personally. Don't. Because as much as you'd like to believe it's true, it's not always about you. Don't assume people are only talking about you and your failures. They are not. Contrary to what you think, people have little time to dwell on your failures, or your successes for that matter. They are busy in their own lives and have moved on long ago, so should you.

I know sometimes you feel alone and different. But don't let being different hold you back. I am often the only brown woman in a room full of white women. What's more, I am often the only brown woman in a room full of black women. In both cases, people often ask: "Don't you feel like the odd one out?" I don't. In fact, I consider myself the special one in! Do not be afraid to be the only one in the room. Don't lose your voice and your identity just to 'fit in' with the crowd. Stepping up requires even more courage when you are in a new culture and environment or when you are in a minority. But that's OK. No one said it will be easy. From a person who has had to relocate twice and start her business from scratch twice, my advice to you out there is to step up, show up and never be afraid to ask for opportunities. Even if you are refused, try again later. You won't get anything if you don't ask for it and don't persist long enough.

The journey to the top will take a different form for each individual over the course of time. But know that whether you cover your head or not, whether you belong to this side of the wall or the other, whether you are born in this country or have immigrated, whether you are black, brown or white, it doesn't and it shouldn't matter; let no one tell you what you can and cannot do. You are compassionate. You are smart. You are capable. No matter how many challenges come your way, the power to rise above all challenges and crush all stereotypes lies within you. Last but not least, know that we are in this together and together we can make it to the top.

 Advancing Your Potential

 @advancingyou

 Giving Wings To Your Potential

 @advancingyou

(in) Hira Ali

Don't forget to register at www.advancingyourpotential.com where you will find free trainings and activities related to the book under the tab – *Her Way To The Top*.

REFERENCES

CHAPTER 1

Nice Girls Don't Get the Corner Office - Lois Frankel

Lean In - Sheryl Sandberg

The Confidence Code - Katty Kay & Claire Shipman

Why We Need To Ditch "Fix The Women" Solutions - Michelle King, Thrive Global

The 'Female Confidence Gap' Is a Sham - Jessica Valenti, Guardian

Is the Confidence Gap Between Men and Women a Myth? - Laura Guillen, HBR

Women Fast Forward - How Long until Gender Parity? - Ernst & Young

Girls' Attitudes Survey 2014 - Girl Guiding

Index of Leadership Trust - Institute Of Leadership & Management

Women Don't Ask - Linda Babcock

The American Association of University Women Survey

The Secret Thoughts of Successful Women - Valerie Young

The Power of Vulnerability - Brené Brown TEDx talk

Listen to Shame - Brené Brown TEDx talk

Unlocking The Full Potential Of Women At Work - McKinsey

Minority Women Really Are Least Likely To Be Promoted In Corporate America - Georgene Huang

Men aren't holding us back – we're doing it ourselves - Liz Jones

'Make Failure Your Fuel.' Read Soccer Star Abby Wambach's Barnard Commencement Address - Katie Reilly

Your Body Language May Shape Who You Are - Amy Cuddy TEDx talk

CHAPTER 2

What's the Psychology Behind the Fear Of Missing Out? - Anita Salz, Clinical Psychologist

Do you know how to switch off? - Psychologies

The Heartbreaking Way FOMO Fuels Working Mom Guilt - Sara

The National Parenting Association Survey

High Octane Women: How Super Achievers Can Avoid Burnout - Sherrie Bourg Carter

Motherhood versus Career, The Epic Battle That Need Not Be - Sherrie Bourg Carter

Why motherhood needs to be more compatible with having a career - Sarah Biddlecombe

Why do so few German mothers go back to work? - Katinka Barysch

Women in Pakistan's workforce - The Nation

Study conducted by the National Institute of Child Health and Human Development (NICHD)

We can't have it all - former *Vogue* editor-in-chief Alexandra Shulman on why she thinks women are setting themselves impossible standards, *Daily Mail*

No, We Can't Have It All - Douglas Rushkoff

Mom Fomo - Latte and Love

Girl Boss - Sophia Amoruso

CHAPTER 3

CHAPTER 4

What Women Can't Let Go - Julia Edelstein

Never Done: A History of American Housework - Susan Strasser

Dear Women, Find Pride In Your Flaws, In The Dusty Elements Of Your Being - Kadambari Srivastava

Getting Past Perfect: How to Find Joy and Grace in the Messiness of Motherhood - Kate Wicker

Daring Greatly - Dr Brené Brown

CHAPTER 5

Women and Time: Setting a New Agenda - Real Simple/Families and Work Institute (FWI) survey

What Makes Us Tick - Ruth Davis Konigsberg

Women 'better at multitasking' than men, study finds - James Morgan, science reporter, BBC

Melinda Gates explains why 'time poverty' is one of the biggest challenges of the modern era - Olga Khazan, The Atlantic

Personal Leadership Training Guide - Dan Gregory

Time Poverty, Work Status and Gender: The Case of Pakistan - Najam us Saqib Pakistan & GM Arif

You Are Allowed To Have Boundaries With Family - Natalie

Work Simply: Embracing the Power of Your Personal Productivity Style - Carson Tate

Getting Things Done - David Allen

CHAPTER 6

Brag: How to Toot Your Own Horn Without Blowing It - Peggy Klaus

Let's Roar! How to Promote Yourself without Sounding Arrogant - International Association for Women

This Is Not the Career I Ordered - Caroline Dowd-Higgins

Personal Rebranding: How To Be Seen Differently - Caroline Ceniza-Levine

How to promote yourself without sounding arrogant - sponsor content from National Association of Professional Women

Reinventing You - Dorie Clark

10 Ways To Brag About Yourself Without Sounding Like A Jerk - John Corcoran

Self-Deprecating Humour is Linked to Wellbeing, study finds - Helen Smith

How to Talk About Yourself Without Sounding Cheesy - Esther Stanhope

CHAPTER 7

The Strength of Vulnerability - The Girl's Lounge Medium

The Power of Vulnerability: Why Women Should Embrace Their Softer Side - Rawper

News & Insights about Closing the Leadership Gender Gap - Why Women-Only Leadership Programs? Congratulations! - Susan L. Colantuono

Professional women lose confidence and ambition as they reach mid-career - new Bain & Company study

Women & Emotional Vulnerability - Anna Leksa

Yes, Being Vulnerable Is Terrifying - But Here's Why It's So Worth It - Katherine Schreiber

Too Close For Comfort: Exploring the Risks of Intimacy - paperback, 12 July 2001, Geraldine K. Piorkowski

7 Ways to Let Yourself Become More Vulnerable - Marlen Komar

Evolution of the Self - Leon F. Seltzer PhD

The Power to Be Vulnerable - Sylvia Ann Hewlett & Norma Vite-Leon, High-Achieving Women, 2001 (New York: National Parenting Association, 2002)

Study of Early Childcare and Youth Development - National Institute of Child Health and Human Development

High Octane Women: How Super Achievers Can Avoid Burnout - Sherrie Bourg Carter

I Am Not Your Guru, Documentary - Tony Robbins

Could you benefit from being more authentic in the workplace? - Jenny Garrett

Daring Greatly - Brené Brown

CHAPTER 8

How To Beat Decision Fatigue With Better Brain Habits - Janet Mesh

Coping strategies to overcome personal and professional challenges - what you can do to help you move forward - Kalyani Pardeshi

The Cure for Decision Fatigue - Choosing not to make choices might be the best response to the daily avalanche of options - Jim Sollisch

The Female Face of Poverty - Fifty years after the War on Poverty began, millions of women are still struggling to get by - Maria Shriver

CHAPTER 9

Minority Women Really Are Least Likely To Be Promoted In Corporate America - Georgene Huang

Laughing All the Way to the Bank - Fabio Sala

CHAPTER 10

Still just a bit of banter? Sexual harassment in the workplace in 2016 - Trades Union Congress

My boss sexually harassed me at the work Christmas party. What should I do? - Louisa Symington-Mills

Sexual Harassment in the Workplace Defined - Rebecca Berlin

Examples of Sexual Harassment - Alison Doyle

EU Commission Code of Practice on Measures to Combat Sexual Harassment - Slater & Gordon Lawyers, UK Press Releases

Workplace Harassment - What It is and What to Do About It – Velsoft

CHAPTER 11

Today is Equal Pay Day: from now, women work 'for nothing' - Emelia Murray

1918 vs 2018: 13 things women couldn't do 100 years ago - Mark Molloy, Jamie Johnson, Izzy Lyons

Upskirting row: MP's office targeted in 'pants protest'

World Economic Forum (WEF), in the Global Gender Gap Report 2017

Caroline Criado Perez: How I put a suffragist in Parliament Square - Nicci Gerrard

Equality is a men's issue too - Emma Watson's UN speech

Both men and women have to address gender inequality - British Council

How To Campaign For Women's Rights: 8 Steps You Can Take To Tackle Gender Inequality In 2017 'Women's rights are human rights' - Natasha Hinde

ABOUT THE AUTHOR

Leadership Trainer, Motivational Speaker, Writer, Executive Career Coach and licensed Neuro Linguistic Programming (NLP) Practitioner.

Hira is a multi-faceted coach who has impacted hundreds of people from various industries and professions across the world. From teachers to students, executives to police officers, business owners to corporate career women, her client base is diverse, and her commitment to helping everyone achieve their highest potential is unwavering. With outstanding client reviews of 98%, it's clear her clients find tremendous value in Hira's unique approach.

Hira's success as a professional coach is grounded in the belief that human potential is infinite. Helping others become the best version of themselves has been the most rewarding aspect of her career. It's also enabled her to connect intellectually and emotionally with incredible individuals from a variety of backgrounds – people who have unlimited potential and just needed a focused guide to help them unlock it.

Hira is an Associate Certified Coach accredited by International Coach Federation and a professional member of the Association for Neuro Linguistic Programming. Her widely acclaimed leadership and coaching articles have been featured across a variety of leading outlets: *The International Coach Federation*, *The Huffington Post*, *Thrive Global*, *Women @ Forbes*, *Ellevate Network* and many more. Her recent blog on overcoming self-doubt and Impostor Syndrome was published on *Thrive Global*, shared by Arianna Huffington, and then retweeted, liked and endorsed by thousands in less than 24 hours. Her career development podcast, *8 Minutes of Learning With Hira Ali*, has been featured in *HuffPost* as one of the top 100 rising podcasts with guests. She has also been featured in several podcast interviews that have inspired listeners across the world and are available on Advancing Your Potential.

Hira is also a registered coach and mentor at various international organisations including: American Corporate Partners, the National Health Trust, Mentor2mentees, and The Cherie Blair Foundation. She was nominated for the prestigious WATC rising star entrepreneur award, and is the recipient of the Top 100 Women – Lift Effects Star Award. She has also been selected as one of the top three finalists for the Baton Awards, Entrepreneur of the Year. Hira is extremely passionate about empowering and coaching high-performing career women. After training women in Asia, the Middle East, Europe, the US, Canada, and Australia, she earned the title of International Coach & Trainer for Women in Leadership. In *Her Way to the Top: A Guide to Smashing the Glass Ceiling*, she highlights the career challenges women face globally and the cultural implications of these challenges.

Those concepts and the strategies to overcome them are also reviewed in her new online women's leadership program Career Excel. Career Excel is a comprehensive online leadership training program available to help women achieve their professional potential through live coaching, global networking, and an in-depth curriculum. The program aims to empower women to be fearless at work, home and in life.

*If you are ready to move to the next level and wish to be better positioned to effect change in your career then be sure to visit www.careerexcel.us

For free trainings and activities related to the book, don't forget to register yourself at www.advancingyourpotential.com

You got this! See you there!

Printed in Great Britain
by Amazon

76279863R00132